SIDEWALK STRATEGIES

Seven Winning Steps for Candidates, Causes and Communities

Larry Tramutola

SIDEWALK STRATEGIES

ISBN: 0-9744668-2-4

Some of this book has appeared elsewhere in slightly different form. The Cabrillo Village story was first published as part of Remembering Cesar published by Quill Driver Press.

To order books singly or in bulk direct from TRAMUTOLA:
Tel: 510.658.7003
Fax: 510.658.7302
E-mail: info@tramutola.com
Web: www.TRAMUTOLA.com or www.SIDEWALKSTRATEGIES.com

Published by

TurnKey
press

2525 W Anderson Lane, Suite 540
Austin, Texas 78757

Tel: 512.407.8876
Fax: 512.478.2117
E-mail: info@turnkeypress.com
Web: www.turnkeypress.com

To Ann—for her love, humor, spirit and brilliance.

Contents

Acknowledgements

I wasn't able to ask Fred Ross Sr. who taught him how to organize; he died before I had the chance.

Fred, the greatest teacher of organizing, must have had a mentor. If he did, he or she is nameless. Perhaps Fred learned how to empower people by trial and error, by making mistakes and by learning from them.

For those of us who followed, we are indebted to him. Fred was our mentor. His lessons inspired us to do something with our lives beyond making money.

I wish Fred had written his book about organizing. If he had it would have saved me the task and it would have been much better.

* * * * *

Many people contributed to this book, some knowingly, others unknowingly. I am indebted to my father and my grandfather who taught me important lessons about hard work and honesty, and the importance of family.

Dolores Huerta and Cesar Chavez were invaluable role models who devoted their lives to a cause greater than themselves. Other organizers, not so famous but equally talented have been colleagues and contributors and I have learned from each of them: Bob Lawson, Marshall Ganz, Jim Drake, Scott Washburn, Richard Ross and Eliseo Medina.

I would like to thank Jane Norling, colleague and artist extraordinaire, for her illustrations and artwork that we have used in many of our campaigns; and Dave Wenger for suggesting that my stories about organizing could grow into a book, and for being so wise and helpful throughout the process.

I am deeply indebted to friends and family who read and re-read the manuscript and made important and thoughtful suggestions: Bonnie Moss, Charles Heath, David Basmajian, David Chilenski, Tom Balawejder, Reuben Weinzveg, Bruce Cain, David Averbuck and my first teacher, my mother, Barbara Tramutt.

Special thanks to Julia Gordon who not only read and edited the book numerous times, but also patiently provided the glue that kept everything together. I am deeply appreciative of my many friends who, upon reading the first printed version of the book, provided feedback, encouragement and smart edits and corrections.

Thanks to the following people at TurnKey Press and Phenix & Phenix: Andy Morales, Courtney McAnalley, Katy Powell, Ryan Myers and Jennifer Berry.

Thanks to my children: Jennifer, Mike, Cristina and Lena who over the years have listened to too many stories about politics and too few by Dr. Seuss.

Finally, I would like to thank Ann, who has traveled with me every step of the way on our life's journey. Her insightful suggestions and encouragement, not just in writing this book, but throughout our life together, have made me a better writer, organizer and most important of all, a better husband and father. While I learned from many great teachers, I learned the most from her.

An old man going on a lone highway,
Came at the evening, cold and gray,
To a chasm vast and deep and wide
Through which was flowing a sullen tide;
The old man crossed in the twilight dim,
The sullen stream held no fears for him;
But he turned when safe on the other side
And built a bridge to span the tide.

"Old man," said a fellow pilgrim near,
You are wasting strength with building here,
Your journey will end with the ending day;
You never again will pass this way,
You have crossed the chasm deep and wide,
Why build you this bridge at the eventide?"

The builder lifted his gray head,
"Good friend, in the path I have come," he said.
"There followeth after me today
A youth whose feet must pass this way
This chasm that has been naught to me,
To that fair-haired youth may a pitfall be;
He too must cross in the twilight dim,
Good friend, I am building the bridge for him."

Anonymous

Introduction

Local elections for city councils, school boards and local tax measures are often viewed as "low interest" elections. Successful local candidates rarely make the national news or get interviewed on CNN, and the results from school bond elections or local tax measures are not usually reported on the front page of newspapers or on the evening TV news. But the people we elect in these local elections, and whether or not citizens vote to approve school or other tax measures, more directly affect the quality of our lives and the quality of our communities than elections for senators or presidents. Local elections deal with vital community needs from repairing roads to renovating schools. They determine who governs our local schools, our public hospitals and our transit systems.

While most other political consultants strive to work on "bigger" or "more important" elections, I believe that local elections are the key to successful communities. Local elected officials make decisions regarding land uses, and they decide where new homes, schools and roads will be built. Local officials determine zoning rules that affect the quality of local neighborhoods, and they decide what businesses and jobs come into communities. The public, by approving or rejecting tax measures, determines the quality of roads, local schools, recreational facilities, libraries and emergency services. "Quality of life issues," which include traffic, education and health care choices, are all affected by local elections.

My company has won over 400 local elections from California to South Carolina, from conservative communities like Orange County, California, to liberal San Francisco. Today our firm is one of the most successful political consulting firms in the country. We have elected mayors, city council members, state and national officials. We have passed billions of dollars in tax measures in suburbia, the inner city, mountain areas and farm country. We have helped tiny one-school school districts as well as some of the largest public school districts in the country. We have helped improve colleges and hospitals, parks, libraries, museums, zoos and public transit systems. Our successes have not come easily. There were no textbooks or manuals to guide us. I was fortunate, however, to have great teachers and role models who believed that through organizing people and working hard you could improve the world.

When I began organizing fresh out of college I was full of idealism but lacked any practical experience. I was eager to make my life relevant by making a difference in the world but had no idea where to start. I decided to volunteer to help the United Farm Workers union (UFW), led by Cesar Chavez. I thought I would spend a few months helping and then move on. I ended up working with Cesar Chavez and the UFW for almost 11 years and 19 more years doing other community and political organizing. The lessons I learned in the UFW provided the foundation for my career as a political organizer. Over the years that followed I learned other valuable lessons from other skilled organizers and by trial and error.

When I joined the UFW it was struggling for survival in its attempt to improve the lives of America's poorly paid agricultural workers. My contribution to the "cause" in the early years was standing out in front of grocery stores asking people to not purchase grapes or lettuce. For hours on end, we would talk to shoppers hoping we could convince them to support the farm workers. It was hard work, but I learned how to approach people, how to express passion in a few moments, how to be positive when you are tired and the importance of incremental progress. While others went to graduate school or law school, I learned about people on the sidewalks in front of supermarkets.

The strategies I learned on the sidewalks and through successes and failures in hundreds of campaigns have been distilled into seven key strategies—I call them *Sidewalk Strategies*™. These strategies are the foundation for effective political organizing and include the following:

- **Working for what you believe in.** Effective political action begins with personal commitment. What is your personal motivation? What do you care about? Understanding your own motivation is the first step toward winning.

- **Developing discipline.** Success comes from hard work over long periods of time. Do you have it in you to be successful and to put in effort day after day after day? Are you motivated to spend your time working while others are playing? How do successful people develop the discipline to be successful?

- **Knowing how to win.** Wanting to win is nice, but knowing how to win is better. What are the rules you need to follow (or break) to be successful? How do you use time, money and people successfully?

- **Listening.** How do you learn what the public wants? How do you turn that knowledge into your advantage and your political success?

- **Defining the debate.** Simplicity, clarity and repetition are the keys to successful communication. Is your message simple and clear? How do you get your message heard by those who need to hear it? How do you stay focused on your message?

- **Investing in people.** Successful campaigns are built by people. How do you find good people, and how can you create an environment where they can be effective?

- **The willingness to keep working, win or lose.** Successful political activists must deal with failure and setbacks. Do you have the ability to keep going when things are tough or difficult? What did you learn? How do you keep positive in the face of disappointments?

Sidewalk Strategies—Seven Winning Steps for Candidates, Causes and Communities, is written to provide practical lessons on how to win and how to inspire people. It is written for young people struggling with what to do with their lives. And it is written for those that want to be successful electorally, whether or not they have an interest in running for office. Using the strategies that I have learned over many years, I will show you the important steps to elect quality people and how to improve your neighborhood and your community. You will learn how to get people to vote for tax increases to help fund improvements for schools, hospitals, libraries and roads. Most importantly, you will discover how to use organizing techniques to be effective politically. You may be inspired to run for office yourself.

Electing good local candidates and getting people involved in their community takes hard work. It is sometimes difficult to even get people to vote. Some people believe voting will not make a difference and that voting is meaningless. Yet, just a few votes may be the margin between a successful measure to improve a school district or the continual deterioration of schools. Just a few votes may decide who is elected judge or mayor or who is elected to serve on the city council or school board or health district. Voting does make a difference, and this book will provide practical lessons on getting people to vote.

* * * * *

Many of our citizens say they are "turned off" by politics and politicians, yet local political campaigns offer citizens, young and old, the opportunity to participate and be effective in the political process. Volunteers who are inspired to participate in local campaigns bring vitality and energy to our political system. Their efforts on behalf of schools, libraries, hospitals and colleges — and the people who are elected to serve on local boards, councils and commissions — breathe energy and life into our political system and our local communities.

There are predictable steps to winning local elections and organizing people. With proper guidance, coaching and encouragement, you *can* win. Our approach works. It works with candidates, it works for issue elections, and it works at every level of grassroots organizing. We have been successful over 95% of the time, even though most of the elections we are involved in have required a super majority (55% or 67%) of the vote to win. Many of our successful clients had previously lost before hiring us, some as many as five times. By teaching them the *Sidewalk Strategies*, they became successful.

So whether you are a college student looking to make a meaningful difference or someone that cares about your community, the first step towards winning is to discover what it is that moves you, what you are passionate about, what you believe in. Let's get started.

"Do you want to be a positive influence in the world? First, get your own life in order. Ground yourself in the single principle so that your behavior is wholesome and effective. If you do that, you will earn respect and be a powerful influence.

Your behavior influences others through a ripple effect. A ripple effect works because everyone influences everyone else. Powerful people are powerful influences. If your life works, you influence your family.

If your family works, your family influences the community.

If your community works, your community influences the nation.

If your nation works, your nation influences the world.

If your world works, the ripple effect spreads throughout the cosmos.

Remember that your influence begins with you and ripples outward. So be sure that your influence is both potent and wholesome.

How do I know this works?

All growth spreads outward from a fertile and potent nucleus. You are a nucleus."

Lao Tzu

SIDEWALK STRATEGY #1

WORK FOR WHAT YOU BELIEVE IN

It has been said that the most difficult step in any journey is the first step. To win politically, the first step is to have an understanding of your own motivations. What do you want to accomplish? How will your community be better if you win? How will your journey to be politically successful help or empower others? Is your motivation personal or is it based in deeper values? To win you must start with a self-examination of your own motivations for winning.

If you want to win politically because you are interested in personal power or becoming rich, then this book is not for you. It is for the person who wants to win because they want to do something productive with their life and who wants to make the community better. It is for the person who sees a problem and wants to fix it, a person who can't be quiet when they hear of injustice or inequities, a person who wants to win because losing means a deterioration of their community.

Before you can win, you must know *why* you want to win. The first Sidewalk Strategy is to work for what you believe in.

When I started organizing I wasn't sure what I believed in. I was young, idealistic and had little life experience. To become effective, I had to discover my own motivations and I had to overcome the pressures of family and peers in order to do something that I felt was meaningful with my life. Today many young people are struggling with the same pressures of making a living or finding a job. Being able to do something worthwhile with their lives seems difficult and remote.

Chapter One: "What do you care about?" explores what it takes to pursue the unconventional path. Chapter Two is about taking the time and effort to determine what you want to accomplish. Before embarking on a political career, or before asking the community for a tax increase, you must answer the question: How will my efforts make things better?

Chapter Three discusses the importance of commitment. Without commitment, achieving success is impossible. Commitment is learned over time through success and through failure, but mostly by keeping at it.

It is possible to make a difference in the world, and it all starts with the first Sidewalk Strategy: Work for what you believe in.

Chapter One

What Do You Care About?

About once a year, I am asked to speak to a political science class at the University of California at Berkeley. It is a large class—250-300 juniors and seniors. Their questions are always interesting and often insightful. Barely 20 years old, the students are nevertheless struggling with career and life choices. Almost half of them raise their hands when I ask how many are planning to go to law school. They laugh nervously or smile when I suggest they are perhaps planning to attend law school, not because they are interested in the law, but rather to satisfy their parents or to postpone serious decisions about what they want to do with their lives.

Occasionally, a few students have clear career paths identified. They listen then go on their way. Most students, however, are really searching. Still idealistic, they have not had enough life experience to become cynical or overwhelmed with responsibilities. A handful of students come up to talk to me afterwards and ask how they can get involved in politics. Some are bold enough to say they want to run for office, and I ask them: "why?"

"Well I just do, I think it would be cool," is a typical response.

Then I ask them: "What do you believe in?" or "What do you care about that you would be willing to invest your life doing?" They struggle for answers. The questions are not easy, and there are no easy answers. I encourage the students to take an unconventional path and consider postponing going to law school or graduate school.

"Take time to *volunteer* for a cause you believe in," I tell them. "Do something that requires both *disciplined hard work* and *working with people*."

The words "volunteer" and "hard work" usually weed out the students who are just looking to improve their résumés. Those who are scared off by volunteering or hard work are probably not too interested in improving the world and will probably not make very good elected officials. Some students have already bought into the idea that a job with an investment banking firm or a corporate law firm is more important than volunteering to help inner city kids learn to read. Others are eager to begin cashing paychecks. I suggest to them that at this point in their lives, gaining life experience is more important than a paycheck.

A few listen when I challenge them to get involved in something meaningful. I try to be encouraging *and* realistic. I tell them that the only reason to get involved in politics is to work for people and causes that will make a difference. I also caution them to be prepared to have their friends and family attempt to talk them out of it.

"Politics is such an ugly career!" someone who never votes will suggest.

"You'll never make any money!" suggests another.

I have recruited and trained hundreds of young people to work in politics or unions or community work, and regrettably, only a few had supportive families when they started. Virtually all of them had to struggle with what their parents wanted them to do, and what they themselves felt compelled to do.

When I started working with the UFW I was 22 years old, barely out of college. My decision to "volunteer" for the UFW was not popular with my parents. Despite growing up in a very close and supportive family, my desire to become an activist and an organizer did not sit well with my parents, who had sacrificed significantly to send me to college. The Second World War had forced my father to change his plans of becoming a doctor, as he was almost 30 when the war ended, and he was finally discharged from the army. My parents felt "wasting time" by volunteering, even for a meaningful cause, would affect other important life decisions.

"What about your future? You need to save for retirement."

"You went to one of the best universities in the country, you're wasting your education."

"No one will ever want to marry you. You've got no income, no future!"

I had no good answers about my future, who I would marry or even a clue how I would deal with retirement. But at 22, I believed I had many years to figure this out. I didn't have a clear career path, but I knew what I did not want to do. I was not interested in a 9 to 5 job or climbing up the corporate ladder. Many of my friends had jobs that were well-paying, but they did not care who they were working for or what they were doing as long as they got paid. That was not for me. I was a product of the '60s—concerned with Civil Rights, the Vietnam War and social justice. The future, I thought, would take care of itself, and so, either wisely or foolishly, I decided to do "my own thing."

It was a hard decision, and for a number of years, it created a barrier between my family and me. At family functions we discussed sports not politics. When questions like money, retirement, providing for family or the future came up, we disagreed and moved on. During one family get-together, my mother asked me exasperatedly, "Well just what should I tell my friends? What do I tell them when they ask me what you are doing?"

I said, "Tell them the truth. Tell them that I am working for the farm workers who are among the most exploited workers in the world. Tell them that unless people like us do something about it, they will continually be exploited."

"But it would be a lot simpler to tell them you're an attorney," she said.

"Precisely, but I'm not and I won't be. I can have a bigger impact doing what I'm doing."

When college friends, who had taken jobs with investment companies or multinational corporations, heard that I was working for virtually no pay they laughed and said, "You could make more money painting houses!" They were right and there were times when the lack of money and the things that money provides made life difficult.

Pursuing a non-conventional career path is not easy. Do not expect a lot of support from friends and family. If you get it, you are one of the lucky ones.

Today I have my own family, and while none of my children are likely to choose a career in politics or organizing, I encourage them to explore, take risks, do something with their lives that will make a difference and not worry about a paycheck. If they do not take risks when they are young, when will they do it? Careers seldom work out as planned, and a person is better off trying something and learning something rather than taking the safe path to satisfy others.

I tell students: "Respect your parents but don't let them live your life." I advise them to take time to think about what they believe in and what they would like to spend their lives doing. To be successful in politics or organizing, you need to have practical life experience and not just a good résumé or academic experience. To gain that experience, you need to work for what you believe in, even if it means little or no pay.

I receive calls all the time from people who are looking to get involved in politics or community organizing. The best way to get started is to volunteer and local campaigns are a great place to start.

Campaigns and organizations are always looking for talented people who will work for free. Volunteer at a campaign answering phones or organizing a mailing. At every opportunity, volunteer to go door-to-door to talk to voters or collect signatures on petitions in shopping centers. You will learn how to approach people and to communicate simply and quickly. Whatever you do, be serious about your volunteer effort. The more time you can commit the better—three evenings a week, every Saturday, twice a week during the day. The choice is yours, but whatever you commit to, be consistent and reliable. There will be countless opportunities to take additional responsibility. When the opportunity comes along, jump at it.

Getting started in politics is easier than you might think, and it is not just for the young. In every community there are at least two election cycles: November elections and primary or local elections. Determine what races might be interesting—interesting because the race is competitive—interesting because of the person who is running—interesting for any number of reasons. Determine if there is any race that interests you enough to *volunteer*. If so, make contact with the campaign. Tell them you have "X" amount of time and would like to help this person get elected. Ask if there is anything *they* want done that you can help with. Do not be picky. You might be making calls to voters one night, and soon, you may be asked to coordinate the phone bank. If you work hard, you might be asked to work full-time on the campaign soon thereafter. Good campaign workers are often asked to become staff once their candidate is elected.

Most importantly, do what you love. Get involved to make a difference, not to make a name for yourself or to earn a salary. Do not get involved in politics or community organizing because of the glamour or excitement because there is not much. Political work is hard work, and it takes incredible discipline and sacrifice to be successful. If you are interested in having weekends off and short workdays, it is definitely not for you. If you do not love it, you will not want to volunteer to work in the evenings or on Saturdays when your friends are hanging out or doing something fun. Often, it is the "extra work," the work on evenings and weekends, that leads to success.

Success is usually the result of effort applied over a long period of time to a specific target. Successful political organizing has been likened to digging a hole with a shovel. One person consistently digging shovel after shovel full of dirt will eventually dig a hole. Several people digging shovel full by shovel full will accomplish more, and many people digging will create even bigger results. Often, it is just hard work done over days and days that yields significant results.

Be prepared to deal with losses and failures. If you have a "thin skin" or cannot handle some defeats or criticism, you are too sensitive to have a career in politics. Successes and failures are public. When you win, everybody is a fan. When you lose, everyone is a critic.

If you are interested in getting involved in politics or community organizing, work *only* for people and causes that you *really* believe in. If you do not care about the candidate or cause, chances are you will not put in the extra effort required to be successful. Like exercise, it is the extra effort that yields improvement.

Be positive. Nothing is more debilitating to others than to be around a person who has a negative attitude. Part of being positive is being a role model for others. Never think you are too important to walk a precinct or call voters. This is true for both volunteers and candidates. The more of it you do, the more you will learn. Often the most important work is the least glamorous, but whatever you do, be positive. Set the example for others.

To put in the effort it takes to be successful, you must know what you believe in and why you want to win. The foundation of successful organizing is working for something more important than yourself. If you know why you want to win and you have patience, discipline and a positive work ethic, you have a good chance of being successful.

Chapter Two

Why Do You Want to Win?

I have been interviewed hundreds of times by political candidates seeking a political strategist and by public institutions seeking to pass a tax measure in their community. Depending on the level of the campaign, the office sought, or the importance of the election, and the potential budget, the interview process can be fairly informal or quite formal. Prospective consultants often prepare elaborate presentations complete with sample mail, clever TV spots, examples of attacks on the opposition and testimonials from previous successful clients. A campaign with money has its pick of political consultants, and most consultants are more than eager to do whatever is necessary in order to land a client.

While the public and the press may hold political consultants in low esteem, anyone who wants to win at the ballot wants a warrior on their side who will lead them to an election victory. Consequently, the interview process usually focuses on the "how's" of getting elected:

- How the campaign will be conducted.
- How to raise money.
- How to neutralize the opposition.
- How to communicate the campaign message.

There is one question that is rarely asked during the interview, but it is the most important: *Why* do you want to win?

A number of years ago, I decided that I would try to switch roles in the interview process. Instead of being interviewed by a potential client, I would interview them—a practice I continue today. I want to know what motivates them and what they care about. I attempt to discover their real motivations for wanting to win or for running for office. Sometimes it works, sometimes it does not. Over the years I have learned that no amount of makeup can hide the flaws of a poor candidate, and the worst candidates are those who have no good reasons as to why they are running for office. Issue campaigns are the same way. If the proponents of a ballot measure are not able to clearly and simply articulate why they need public support and how the community will be improved, there is little chance the measure will pass.

During my interviews I like to look a potential candidate in the eyes and ask: "Why do you want to win?" I am usually disappointed when I ask that question because, unfortunately, few have taken the time to really think about why they want to win.

The answers vary:

"Well, hmmm, I've always wanted to be a leader."

"I think I'd like to be in Washington (or Sacramento)."

"I'd like to be a Senator some day, and this is a good place to start."

"My union/pastor/friends/family encouraged me to run."

Some recite some canned superficial phrase:

"I want to bring dignity to American families."

"I'll fight crime."

My experience has been that most people who run for office have not developed a clear idea of why they are running or what they want to accomplish once they are in office. Because of this, they often have a difficult time articulating a vision. A person who can clearly articulate why she wants to be elected and what she wants to accomplish in office, has a much greater chance of being elected. More importantly, she also has a better chance of being effective once in office.

The best candidates often are those who are motivated to run for office, not because they are ambitious politically but because they are already involved in local activities that demand attention:

- A parent who volunteers at school, frustrated by an ineffective Board of Education.
- A member of a local Neighborhood Watch program fed up with crime in her neighborhood.
- An activist upset with poorly planned developments.

Unfortunately, most potential candidates are usually more interested in *how* they can win than *why* they should win. They want to learn *how* to use the right political strategies and techniques, *how* to spend their financial resources, and *how* we will manage their campaign.

Before I answer their questions, I ask, "*Why* do you want to be elected? *What* do you want to accomplish when you are elected? *Why* should people vote for *you*?" I try to find out what they care about and what they have volunteered to help with in their free time.

At a party I recently attended, I found myself sitting next to a host of a popular morning TV talk show. Our conversation eventually turned to politics and politicians, and the talk show host pointed to a young man and said, "He should go into politics, he's got it all—charisma, good looks. He is a charmer. He'd look good on TV." Her comments intrigued me. *Is this what the media looks for in a candidate?* I suggested that perhaps we should encourage people to run for office who have other qualities and that good looks, charisma and charm are over valued, and qualities like being able to listen, to work hard and to organize others are far more important qualities.

Encouraging people to run for office is important to our political process. There are numerous formal and informal conferences around the country that cater to those desiring a political career and to those wanting to learn the mechanics of successful campaigning. The audiences vary. Sometimes the attendees are young people looking for advice on how to successfully run for office. Occasionally the conferences target women or ethnic groups with the aim of increasing the number of women or minorities in elective office. Other conferences target school officials who come to learn how to pass tax measures.

The conferences usually cover topics from raising funds to selecting a consultant. Polling and utilizing voter data are frequent topics as are press relations and opposition research. Prospective candidates are coached on how to dress, how to "look" like a candidate and how to write press releases, yet the one topic that should be the lead topic in all of these conferences is rarely discussed: *Why* do you want to win?

I encourage people who are thinking about entering local politics to get involved in community activities. The more a candidate knows about the problems people face in their community, the better prepared she will be to offer solutions. There are opportunities in every community. There are neighborhood watch programs, creek or neighborhood clean ups, Habitat for Humanity, youth recreation programs, schools that need volunteers and local church organizations. Every city has commissions eager for public participation, and many people who serve on local commissions or community boards have had little prior experience.

A candidate for local office should begin his quest with a simple written exercise before he talks to one voter or raises a single dollar. On a sheet of paper write: These are the things I want to accomplish in office: _____. The list should be specific and include categories of goals. It should include things that require voter approval as well as things that can be accomplished though leadership and working with the community. Each goal should have a time as to when it will be accomplished. All goals should be ranked from top to bottom.

When Jerry Brown ran for mayor of Oakland he specifically said that his goal for revitalizing the downtown area would be to encourage housing development that would bring 10,000 more residents to the downtown. Both he and his administration were held accountable for achieving that goal. Ray Nagin, the mayor of New Orleans, won an upset victory by articulating his vision for New Orleans. Staying away from canned, overused sound bites, Nagin simply and effectively told voters what he wanted to accomplish as mayor. Both successful candidates became successful mayors because they knew what they wanted to accomplish and had articulated that vision to voters.

Being an elected official or working in an unelected capacity to improve your community takes a tremendous amount of time and effort. If you do not know why you are doing it or what you want to accomplish or if you lack commitment, you will not stay involved long enough to make a difference.

I learned about commitment from a man named Fred Ross.

Fred Ross Sr. was the best teacher I ever had. Fred trained hundreds of people in community and electoral organizing. What made Fred special was his belief that one person could change the world. Fred thought big. He believed that one person, if he or she could organize others, could stop racism and discrimination and end poverty by building power for poor people. Fred was an optimist who believed a person's life should be spent organizing others.

Ross' most famous disciple and student was Cesar Chavez. Cesar Chavez is now a historical icon, remembered in textbooks and through songs and documentaries. Roads, schools, libraries and parks are named after him. In

California, Cesar Chavez's birthday is a state holiday, and the U.S. government has issued a stamp in his memory. But had it not been for Fred Ross and his ability to teach Cesar the importance of organizing, few people would ever have heard of Cesar Chavez. Even Chavez recognized this: "I learned quite a bit from studying Ghandi, but the first practical steps I learned from the best organizer I know, Fred Ross. He changed my life." Fred changed my life as well.

Chapter Three

What is Your Commitment?

I first met Fred Ross in Salinas, California, "The Lettuce Capital of the World," during the Lettuce Strike in 1970. Ross had retired from a successful career as a community organizer. But Cesar Chavez, the head of the fledgling United Farm Workers, had asked his old mentor to come to Salinas to help organize and train the United Farm Workers' staff. The UFW was beginning a nationwide boycott of lettuce, and the Union planned to send its members and its staff to cities across the country to raise awareness of the farm workers' struggle and to build support for the UFW's lettuce boycott.

I had recently graduated from Stanford and was volunteering at a Legal Aid office hoping to get some first hand knowledge of the law before applying to law school. It was in Salinas where I met Fred—an event that completely changed my life and turned me into a professional organizer.

I arrived in Salinas on a Saturday about midmorning. I had brought a load of donated food to the strikers and their families. After I drove up and parked my VW "squareback" in the ally behind the UFW's office, a half-dozen farm worker women wearing red bandannas came out of the UFW office and helped unload the boxes of canned goods and food from my car. Their children ran in and out of the office while, nearby, several small groups of men, laughing and arguing in Spanish, stood watching us as we came inside.

A meeting was being held in the back corner of the storefront office. The office was cavernous, perhaps a quiet neighborhood grocery store in a former life. But now there was an atmosphere of activity and hustle inside. People were everywhere, standing in groups or sitting against walls on old, battered folding chairs.

I immediately noticed Fred. He was leaning against a wall, his arms folded around a spiral notebook, and he seemed totally out of place. Unlike the farm workers who were mostly in their twenties and thirties, Fred was in his sixties and was tall and lean, with the chiseled looks of an aging Hollywood film star. He was calm and focused, seemingly unaware of the hum of activity in other parts of the large hall. He listened intently as each person, one-by-one, stood up to give their progress report on the strike. Then, I heard him mutter under his breath, "Shit! That guy doesn't know crap about organizing. He's too undisciplined to learn." I asked the person next to me, "Who's the old guy?"

Immediately he replied, "Oh that's Fred Ross, he found and trained Cesar years ago. He's one of the few Anglos that Cesar trusts. He taught Cesar everything about organizing."

Later that evening, quite by chance, I ran into Fred at a Fosters Freeze in town. (I learned later that Fred had a weakness for vanilla shakes.) I introduced myself, said that I had come down for the day to bring food to the strikers, and I had seen him at the UFW office earlier in the day. We spoke a few minutes, and I eventually asked him, "What does it take to be an organizer?"

He looked at me over his glasses and replied, "Time, discipline and hard work. You interested?"

"I might be," I said. He grabbed a stub of a pencil from the pocket of his khaki shirt, scribbled down his name and his San Francisco phone number and said, "If you're interested, give me a call." But as he walked away, he turned and left me with a challenge and a warning of the hard road ahead: "Most don't have it in them to be any good, though."

Despite his less-than-enthusiastic encouragement, I called him on the phone a few days later. I reintroduced myself and told him I had heard that the UFW needed help and that I wanted to learn more. He said he couldn't see me immediately, since he was busy working on a book about Cesar's early organizing days, but he invited me to his house the next day.

When I arrived at his small, sparsely furnished home in the Bernal Heights area in the south end of San Francisco, what struck me at once were the piles of books and yellow notepads, filled with almost illegible writing, scattered around his living room. His desk was piled with stacks of tapes for his portable recorder, and classical music was playing on his ancient record player. We talked for several hours. He spoke thoughtfully, quietly about social justice and activism.

He told stories of organizing Mexican Americans in Los Angeles in the 1950s and running the first successful campaign to elect a Mexican American to the Los Angeles City Council. He talked about the voter registration campaigns he had conducted across the state to increase the political power of minorities. He provided specifics on how the UFW was trying to improve the lives of farm workers and rattled off statistics about the low life expectancy of farm workers and told stories about people caught in poverty who had no hope for the future unless they organized.

His eyes flashed with anger when he talked about police brutality against farm workers. His voice cracked with emotion when he described babies born with deformities due to the use of toxic pesticides.

I listened, stunned with his knowledge and his passion and intrigued as he described his life and successes.

After a while, he stopped talking about himself and his work and began probing me with his piercing, penetrating gaze and words. "Why are you interested in organizing?" he asked.

"Organizing," he said, "is not for everybody, and if you want to be successful, you have to know *why* you are doing it. If you are not committed to something more important than yourself, you'll never be successful."

"Before we talk about organizing," he said, "let's talk about you. What do *you* believe in?"

I was not prepared for this question. I had hoped to talk about the techniques of organizing, and I wanted to hear more stories of how he had organized people. Fred wanted to talk about the "why" of organizing.

I rambled a bit about social justice, civil rights and the antiwar movement. I talked about my own family and how my grandfather had suffered discrimination when he immigrated to the United States, and that my family had actually changed our name to blend in to American society. I told him that in college I had 'sat in' to protest the Vietnam war but I that I felt ineffective. I wanted to make a difference with my life, but I had no idea where to start or what I could do.

Fred said that he had met many people like me who wanted to make a difference, but they lacked the commitment. "Organizing," he said, "is a tough career, and if you can't articulate your own motivation you will have a hard time organizing others."

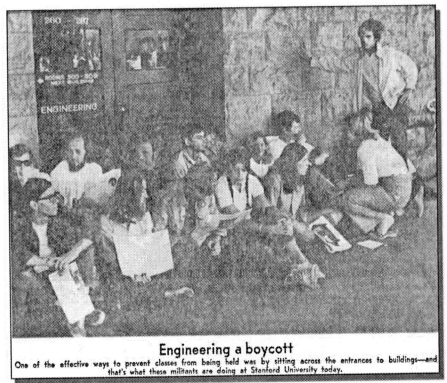

Engineering a boycott

One of the effective ways to prevent classes from being held was by sitting across the entrances to buildings—and that's what these militants are doing at Stanford University today.

Photo reproduced from Palo Alto Times, May 1, 1970

One of my first, and least effective, political acts was "sitting in" in protest of Nixon's bombing of Cambodia during the Vietnam War. It would be years before I learned how to organize effectively.

"I like your honesty," he continued, "and the simple fact that you came to see me may mean that you are serious. When can you start to work? We need people immediately."

"I'm available to help for a few months," I told him. I had no idea at the time that I would stay with the UFW for more than a decade, and the lessons I would learn from him and from others would provide the foundation for a successful career in organizing.

While Fred taught me many lessons about discipline and hard work, strategy and human nature, the most important lesson Fred Ross taught me was to ask the question of myself: What do you care about that you would be willing to invest your life doing? It is a question I ask every person who wants to get involved in politics.

Sidewalk Strategy #2

Develop the Discipline of Winning

Discipline, patience and hard work are the foundation upon which successful political and community organizing is built. Chapter Four revolves around the lessons I learned from Fred Ross Sr., who was an astute student of human nature and a masterful teacher of organizing. Fred was able to break down organizing into a series of practical steps that anyone who had sufficient personal motivation could follow to be successful. From a lifetime of teaching organizing, Fred had observed that discipline was something that could be learned.

Chapter Five is about learning to make progress every day. This *daily* effort is essential for successful organizing. Political success rarely comes easily; it evolves from effort that is sustained over long periods of time. If you want instant gratification or quick results, organizing is not for you.

Chapter Six is about learning to overcome your fears: fear of failure, fear of others, fear of conflict and fear of rejection. Politics and community organizing are not for the faint of heart or the weak of spirit. To make a difference or to bring about change, feathers will need to be ruffled. How one copes with their own fears will determine how successful they will be.

Finally, Chapter Seven deals with the need to develop the "will to win." It is not enough to want to win. Those that win, especially in politics, do not rely on luck or wait for good fortune. Luck may help you win the lottery, but luck plays a small part in winning elections. Developing the discipline to win demands sacrifice, a willingness to take risks, the ability to work hard out of the spotlight and having single-minded focus. Here is how I learned the Discipline of Winning.

Chapter Four

Learning Discipline From the Master

I began learning about organizing from Fred Ross in his cluttered, modest house in San Francisco. As I sat on his floor, he showed me photographs of farm labor camps that could have been from a third world country rather than from areas a few miles south of San Francisco. He showed pictures of himself as a young man celebrating a successful citizenship drive among Mexican immigrants. Each picture told a story and a lesson of a successful organizing drive.

He talked about how he trained people to conduct voter registration drives to increase minority participation in elections so that elected officials would pay attention to minority communities. He talked about all the things that were accomplished—better housing, better schools, improved health care—when people organized themselves. Fred believed that politicians rarely did something worthwhile on their own and that people had to organize themselves if they wanted to improve their communities.

I asked Fred if there was anything written about organizing. "Nothing any good, that's why I'm writing it." (Unfortunately, he never finished his book.)

"Being an organizer takes a tremendous amount of commitment and discipline," he told me, adding that during his life as an organizer, he had found very few people who had the combination of commitment and discipline to be successful, but he was always looking. That was one of the reasons he was writing a book about Chavez's early days organizing the union—to show what Chavez had done to achieve this success.

Lessons of Commitment, Discipline and Hard Work

Since nothing had been written on how to organize, my "learn as you go" training on the job began. My first task was to build community support in Santa Clara County, from San Jose to Palo Alto, for the Union's boycott. I quickly learned that there were no easy steps to follow. My staff consisted of one … me. I was given a few names of local people who had sent money to the Union to support the strike, and from these few contacts, I was asked to build a small army of people who would contribute financially to the Union and support the boycott. My goal was to recruit people to volunteer each week to pass out leaflets about the boycott at grocery stores throughout the county. "The pay is $10 a week," Fred told me, "and you get $100 a month for your rent if you stay more than a month." Luckily, I already had my own car. "The Union will reimburse you for gas," Fred said. "Keep your receipts."

"What about food?" I asked.

"That's what the ten bucks is for. A good organizer will find others to feed him," Fred replied.

"How do I get started?" I asked.

Fred gave me the name of Father Moriarty at the Sacred Heart Church in San Jose.

"Visit him. Tell him what you need. He may help you."

Naively, I started out thinking that all I had to do was share my enthusiasm for the cause, and people would quickly contribute or volunteer; however, I soon found the task of organizing much harder than I had expected. I went to Catholic churches, to schools and unions and got names of potential supporters. But many of the people I called to help me pass out leaflets in front of stores did not show up, and I soon ran out of names to call. I phoned Fred, frustrated and looking for answers. "I'm just not having a lot of success," I told him.

Fred came right to the point, "Of course not. It's hard work and you obviously don't know what you're doing. To be successful, you have to sting people into action. You have to repeatedly prod them to get off their butts."

Fred said I needed to organize myself before I could organize others. When I met him at his house in Bernal Heights a few days later, he had covered his living room wall with a long sheet of butcher paper. On it he had drawn vertical lines creating 14 columns on which he had marked the days of the next two weeks starting with Sunday through Saturday.

Then, he proceeded with his lesson of how to be organized and disciplined.

Fred Ross Sr. was the best teacher I ever had. Fred Ross trained hundreds of people in community and electoral organizing. What made Fred special was his belief that one person could change the world. Fred thought big, he believed that one person, if he or she could organize others, could stop racism and discrimination and end poverty by building power for poor people. Fred was an optimist who believed a person's life should be spent organizing others.

Pointing to the chart and handing me a colored marker, he told me, "Write down everything you have to do each day. Who are you meeting Monday?"

I went over to the butcher paper and wrote down the names and times of the three people that I was supposed to meet that day.

Fred continued, "OK, now when are you calling these people to remind them that you are coming to see them?"

Remind them I was coming to see them? "I hadn't thought of that," I told Fred.

"Well, write that down," he stated firmly. "Reminding is the essence of organizing."

He went over to butcher paper and wrote in the Sunday column: "Make reminder calls to:" Then, he listed the names and phone numbers of the people I was to visit the following Monday.

The lesson continued. "What time are you calling them?" he asked, and before I could answer, he instructed me, "Now write down the time." I did.

But he was not through with me yet. "OK, now on Monday, before you meet with them, you need to call them again, right?" Fred asked.

I just nodded quietly while privately thinking that all this reminding and writing down was a bit of overkill. It was only weeks later that I came to understand that these details, and the discipline to put them into practice, are absolutely essential to good organizing. At the time, though, I had not learned that for myself, and I certainly did not want to challenge Fred, so I said nothing.

Fred went on. "Good. Now write on the butcher paper the time that you plan to call them, so you don't forget. It is always good to call people right before you visit them, so you don't waste time if they are not there."

"And by the way," he continued, "while you are at the house of one of the people on your list, ask if you can use their phone to call your next appointment. That way they'll see how serious you are," he said.

The writing process went on for over two hours, until the butcher paper was covered with notes and reminders. Every hour of the day was accounted for, even sleeping and eating. Fred instructed me, "Estimate how much time you need for each activity—even sleep—and then put an estimated time next to it."

When we were finished, he said, "Now copy everything down in your own notebook, so you have a copy of the schedule and call me each night at 9:00 sharp and report what you have accomplished that day."

As I took out my notebook and began copying, I realized there were no days off. While the week days and evenings were devoted to calling and meeting with people, Friday afternoons and Saturdays were for picketing and leafleting. Sundays were set aside for visiting churches during the day and calling volunteers in the evening, since Sunday evening, I learned, was the best time to call because people were usually home. I even wrote down the times when I was supposed to call Fred each day—"TALK to FRED from 9–11 P.M.," I wrote in big bold letters on each day of the week.

I followed Fred's advice as best I could. Reminding people became essential to achieving success. To do it took discipline and self-organization. Sometimes I did not call people to remind them because I ran out of time or was doing something else and forgot. When that happened, I usually paid the price for my lack of discipline. Sometimes the person was not at home when I arrived at their house to meet with them, or even if they were there, they came to the door and said they could not meet with me.

As he had instructed, I also called Fred each night without fail, though the phone call was torture because he would grill me mercilessly about what I had done. If I was 15 minutes late phoning him, he would call me. "We are supposed to talk everyday at 9:00 not 9:15!"

We started every call with what I had accomplished during the day. He peppered me with probing questions that demanded thoughtful answers and accountability: "Why did you do that?" What did you say when he said that?" The interrogation went on for two hours and often longer, as I had to report and relive my successes and failures of the day. Fred asked me one question after another, and unless I was prepared to simply hang up and walk away from what I was doing, there was no escape or relief. But I endured the torment, partly out of pride and partly because I knew Fred was teaching me invaluable lessons about the importance of follow-through and disciplined work. "There are no short cuts," Fred told me.

No Short-cuts and No Days Off

And so I persevered, week after week of this routine. Why he decided that I was worth taking the time to train I never knew. I did know that the hands on training I was receiving was incredible, even if I was exhausted by the long 14-16 hour days spent trying to meet people, inspire them to participate in picketing or leafleting as well as making my reminder calls so they would show up for meetings or weekend activities. I learned to make appointments with people around dinner time and to graciously accept offers of food. The learning process was slow and I often wondered if I had it in me to be a successful organizer.

I felt raw from Fred's nightly "Inquisition" when he sought to uncover every short cut and mistake I had made during the day. Not only did he call my attention to each flaw, but my admitting I had made a mistake was not enough for him. No, he wanted to know why and what I had learned from that failure.

For instance, after I told him about something I had done wrong, he would ask in an exasperated tone, "Well, *why* did you do that?" When volunteers who had promised to come to help pass out leaflets did not show up, he would say, "I've *told* you that you need to remind people to come. When you are not successful organizing, *you* need to take the responsibility. It is not their fault they didn't show up. It's *yours*. You either didn't do a good enough job inspiring them, or you didn't follow up and let them off the hook. Either way it's your fault."

And then he would give me suggestions in the form of questions on what to do to follow-up with the no-shows to get them to show up the next time. Fred's suggestions were like techniques for getting an escaped fish back on the hook. He would ask me: "Did you call them when they didn't show up? Did you tell them that they were letting you down and, even more importantly, that they were letting the farm workers down?"

His approach was tougher and more grueling than anything I had ever encountered before. When I attended Stanford University, I had taken courses from demanding instructors, and I had tough bosses in my various jobs through school. My own father was a hard taskmaster who required chores and homework to always be done before play. Even so, I was unprepared for Fred's driving intensity. He considered organizing the highest form of community activism. "You have to do it right," he told me. "If you don't, you'll always be blaming something or someone else. Excuses are for failures, and you don't want to fail. Do absolutely everything you can to keep from failing."

So for six months, day after day with no days off, I followed Fred's advice, doing everything he told me. I was determined to succeed.

Finally Some Success

As soon as he felt I had accomplished a task successfully, he demanded more of me. Once I began to successfully organize the one-on-one meetings with potential supporters, he taught me about "house meetings," a more efficient and effective way of reaching people than one-on-one meetings but also more difficult to organize. A house meeting is the opportunity to speak to 14-20 people per night instead of just the two or three you can meet one-on-one. They are much harder to set up because they involve getting someone to host a meeting at their house and getting *that* person to make sure people attend.

Fred explained how to record responses whenever I talked with people—whether in one-on-one meetings or house meetings or for anything else—just like an anthropologist has to keep careful field notes. He showed me how to develop my own call sheets which involved keeping carefully handwritten or typed lists of names, phone numbers and what I said each time I talked to them. (Remember—we were in the "pre-computer" age back then.)

He stressed the importance of telling stories, not fictional stories, but real stories about everyday people and their lives and dreams. "You want to tell stories that illustrate the truth in human terms about poverty, hopelessness, exploitation and racism. You want to tell stories that people can relate to, that they can sympathize and empathize with, so they can put themselves in the shoes of others and feel for them. Stories can inspire people to do something with their own lives to help others."

But most importantly, Fred's repeated statements, reminders and cautions about what to do taught me about discipline. Listen to his litany, repeated again and again:

"Don't assume anything."

"Take responsibility."

"You have to remind people. Reminding people is the essence of organizing."

"Failure is not the result of others not doing things. It is the result of you not organizing correctly."

"Being an organizer requires you to work hours other people don't. That means weekends and evenings. If you are unwilling to do that, you can't be an organizer."

"There are usually two ways to do things, the easy way and the hard way. The hard way is usually best."

The organizing tested me physically, mentally and emotionally. It was a time of many frustrations and few successes. Fred was testing my limits and my commitment.

After a while, his admonitions began to sear firmly into my brain, and eventually, they became a part of my own philosophy. Over time, I began learning my own lessons, which I added to his.

After several months, I began to hear a few words of praise and encouragement as well. Along with the criticisms and admonitions, Fred began to say things like "Good job," or "Hmmm, I guess you have been paying attention." The praise, which had been so rare in the first few months, now became regular, and his encouragement motivated me to work even harder.

I went to college campuses and recruited students to take leaves of absence or take a semester off to work for the UFW. I asked school teachers to work over the summer and nuns to ask permission from their Orders to help. All I could promise them was the $10 a week the UFW offered its organizers, but they were eager to learn, just as I had learned from Fred. In my training sessions with them, I did my best to include the same kind of intense questions and accountability, which Fred had used to grill me. And though I never was as good or as perceptive as Fred, I tried to model my training after his and to give them the best training I could.

I soon found his lessons began to pay off, and my staff grew to three, then six, then twelve. While some left after a few weeks or a few months, unable to handle the personal commitment or discipline, many stayed on, and they became excellent, committed organizers.

Over the years, Fred and I became good friends, but he was always the teacher, and I remained the student. I often called him to ask questions and obtain his insightful advice. I learned to acknowledge my shortcomings and be forthright about my failures.

"Failure," he said, "is part of the learning process. Learn from your mistakes and don't make them again."

Not everyone is cut out to be an organizer, but everyone can make a difference in the world. Success is built upon little steps. As Fred would say: "In organizing, success is built one person at a time, one day at a time. The first person you must organize is yourself. You must know what you believe in, and you must be committed to making a difference. If you can do those things, you will change the world."

All great organizers from Martin Luther King Jr. to Cesar Chavez to

Ghandi are remembered for the *great* things they accomplished—Independence for India, Civil Rights for African Americans, dignity for farm workers—but their success was built on accomplishing little things day after day. To be successful politically you must learn to make progress every day.

Fred Ross died in 1992 at the age of 82 in Marin County, California. His work touched and influenced thousands of people who today fight for social justice, better working conditions and better pay for workers, and an end to violence and war. Although he never finished his book on organizing, his lessons continue to inspire new generations of organizers.

After his death, Fred's son, Fred G. Ross, compiled some of his father's lessons into a small pocket-sized book called "Axioms for Organizers." Here are some of my favorites:

Fred Ross Sr.:

If you are able to achieve anything big in life it's because you paid attention to the little things.

In any other kind of work, if you do a half-assed job at least you get some of the work done; in organizing, you don't get anything done.

When you are tempted to make a statement, ask a question.

Losers are loaded with alibis.

When you are able to take the blame for failure, you are on the way to becoming a good organizer.

Don't waste time fighting the competition; use that time to fight the issues and win. That will take care of the competition.

There is a time for sound and a time for silence, and a good organizer needs to be able to differentiate between the two.

To inspire hope, you have to have hope yourself.

Chapter Five

Make Progress Every Day

If you want to win local elections, forget the glossy campaign flyers, candidate nights and candidate debates. Winning elections takes hard work—getting out and talking to voters about what truly concerns them—and doing it day after day after day.

The process is much the same to what a salesman does to build his territory or what a community policing officer does to get to know her community. In each case, personal contact is absolutely crucial. It is all about meeting people and building relationships through one-on-one phone calls, door-to-door visits and small meetings in people's homes.

But it takes hard work, and it takes time. Whether you are a candidate running for office or an organizer trying to gain support for an issue, you have to make the commitment to work at it "every day," or as I told one candidate running for school board, "every *damn* day." This is a story of how "making progress every day" paid off in a winning campaign.

Bonnie's Story

When I was getting started as a "political strategist," a young woman in her late twenties named Bonnie Moss arrived in my office bubbling with energy. "I'm interested in running for my local Board of Education," she explained. "My friend, who's in the California Legislature, suggested I talk to you."

As she started to hand me her newly printed résumé, I asked about her motivations for running: "Why do you want to serve on the school board?

Do you have children in the schools?" I wanted to know her answers to these questions because I was curious why someone so young should want to serve on the Board of Education, which is often a thankless job.

She hesitated for a moment, as if she did not expect me to ask these questions.

"I want to run because I think I would be good. No, I don't have children, and I'm single. But I have good ideas and work hard. People like me. I think I would do a good job."

I then scanned her resume to see what she had done in the past that might support her claims about having good ideas, working hard, and being liked by others. She was a graduate from a fine women's college and had done some subsequent volunteer work for various community groups—community relations representative, volunteer at the local youth center, president of the Education Foundation. Yet, while she listed her participation in many different activities, nothing really stood out as unique or different. More importantly, nothing set her apart from other competitors who might want to serve on the Board of Education.

I decided to test her knowledge of the school district. I began with what I thought was a simple question: "How many schools are there in the school district?"

She looked surprised, as if no one had ever asked her this before, and she had never thought about the question herself. Finally, as if she felt compelled to give at least some answer, she replied in the form of a question, "Ten?"

"Then, you better find out," I said, knowing she was way off the mark.

Normally, I might not have been interested in helping someone so green and uninformed, even if she had been referred by a friend in the California Legislature. But her eagerness was very likeable, and I wanted to know more about why she wanted to run and what she felt she could contribute to improving her local schools. She spoke about her ideals—wanting to contribute to the community, wanting to make a difference—familiar ideas that I had heard many times before. Yet, she also quite readily admitted that she was new to the political process and emphasized her commitment and enthusiasm. "I'm willing to work hard," she assured me. "I'm willing to learn, and I'll do whatever is necessary to win. Just tell me how."

Finally, I agreed to help her. "But not until you do two things," I said, "and then come back and report on what you learned from each of these things. First, I want you to find out how many schools there are in the district. Then, after you know this, I want you to visit every school. I want you to make appointments to talk with *every* principal and with some teachers at each of the schools to find out what problems they are now facing. And while you're at it, talk to the custodians and secretaries, too. They'll give you an earful!"

She asked, "Every school?"

"Absolutely." I said. "The word will get around that you are visiting schools, and if you don't visit every school, someone will feel offended."

Immediately, she nodded and said, "OK, I get it. I understand."

"When you go to each school, your assignment is to *ask* what is working at the school and what isn't. Just ask questions to learn what's going on, don't try to promote yourself as a candidate." Before she could convincingly ask anyone for their support or their vote, I was hopeful she would learn to listen. Her goal of winning a seat on the Board of Education would start with learning about the schools first hand.

She left saying, "I'll do what you ask." I wasn't sure, however, if I would ever see her again. It's easy to say "Yes" when faced by someone demanding a commitment, just to seem agreeable and likeable. Even if she genuinely intended to do as she said, she might find the assignment daunting and give up. But in a few weeks, to my surprise, she called back to arrange a meeting with me and report on her progress.

When I met her at my office, she proudly announced, "There are 38 schools in the district," answering my first question. She told me she had been visiting the schools. "I've visited 12 of them so far," she said, "and I met with the principal and some teachers at each school, just as you told me. I've also talked to some parents and school custodians. It'll take several more weeks to visit them all. It's a bigger job than I thought, but I'm learning a lot."

I was delighted to hear of her progress and see her willingness to work hard, as she had said she would. It was a good start. Bonnie then proceeded to tell me what she learned. "I learned that most principals had never seen a school board member, since none of the board members ever visit their schools. So when I came to visit, they were actually surprised and happy that a candidate wanted to learn about the schools."

"Very good," I told her. "So what else did you learn?" She went on to describe the appalling conditions she found everywhere. "I learned the schools are in poor shape physically. They are run down on the outside, and classrooms

47

haven't been renovated in years. I even met teachers whose budgets are so tight that they spend their own money for supplies." But she had heard success stories, too. She learned what was working and met teachers who were making a difference by recruiting parents to come into the classrooms to volunteer as aides.

Her school visits made her aware of the surrounding neighborhoods from which the schools drew their students—from the upper middle class areas in the hills, to the ethnic and immigrant neighborhoods in the poorer sections of town.

"Now that you have seen the schools and talked to teachers and principals do you still want to run for the Board?" I asked.

"Most definitely," she said. This time, she responded knowledgeably, no longer just an idealistic political novice. "The schools are in terrible shape. Teachers feel ignored, and children are getting lost. We can do a better job."

She then told me stories of meeting with dedicated principals who were burned out. "They are overwhelmed, unsupported and unappreciated," she concluded. "They feel so frustrated and alienated. I know I'm only one person, but I know I can make a difference."

I agreed to help her in her school board campaign.

She immediately wanted to know all about the strategy and tactics she might use to win. She had dozens of questions: "Can you tell me about candidate nights? What should I say when I go to Rotary meetings and campaign debates? What should my strategy be at political clubs and endorsement meetings?"

"The first thing you should do," I told her, "is forget about candidate nights, debates and endorsement meetings. Your job is to talk to voters, every day … every damn day."

"But," she insisted, "everybody is telling me that the endorsement meetings are crucial."

"I know," I said. "People who don't know what they're talking about will often give advice and most of it is bad. How many of the people who go to these meetings are there because they are interested in what a candidate says?"

She looked uncertain, so I answered the question for her. "Hardly any," I explained. "Each candidate usually packs the audience with his or her supporters, and in the end, the meeting has little impact on undecided voters or the campaign."

I laid out a simple strategy for her to follow. "Every day, I want you to contact a minimum of 35 voters. I want you to do this seven days a week for four months, 122 days."

I told her that my office would provide her with a list of the people most likely to vote, so she would not waste her time, but then it was up to her. "I'll expect you to do your part every day," I told her firmly. "That's every day without fail," I reminded her. You're welcome to go to events if you want but not at the expense of making your calls or visits."

"But what if I can't make those 35 contacts one day?" she asked.

"Then, you have to make up those contacts the next day," I said. "If you make only 25 successful contacts one day, you have to make 45 the next."

I then explained my reason for being so insistent—she had to build up the necessary personal contacts—and she could only do that if she kept at it regularly.

I told her, "If you talk to 35 voters every day, by the end of the campaign, you will have made over 4,000 contacts with real voters, not the people who attend forums and candidate nights."

Lastly, we discussed what she should talk about when she contacted these voters individually. Her goal should be to engage voters about the schools, not promote her candidacy or presumptuously ask voters to support her. "You don't want to ask them to support you yet," I told her. "You want to first show them you are really interested in their issues. Initially, just ask them how they think the schools are doing and what they think works and what doesn't. Take the time to listen. That way, you'll learn more about the schools and voters' attitudes."

To support her efforts, our office sent a piece of mail to every voter she was to call. The letter did not look or feel like a campaign piece. It was a handwritten note from Bonnie along with a short questionnaire asking people their opinion of schools. We hand addressed every one. I am sure her political insider friends were appalled. The letters included tips on helping parents: "Turn off the TV," "Read to your child every night," and "Get to know your child's teacher." We mailed the letters out in small batches every week so Bonnie's calls came on the heels of the letter. Within a couple of weeks, she had received hundreds of completed questionnaires.

As a result of this mailing, her calling became easier. Not only did she have more information about what voters wanted or didn't want, but some people recognized her name from the mailings and complimented her. Occasionally she heard, "Oh, you're the person that sent me that nice letter!" Some voters told her "I really appreciate your concern." But most of all, she

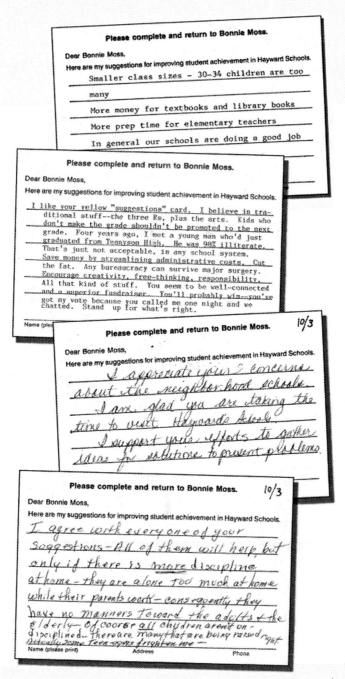

Please complete and return to Bonnie Moss.

Dear Bonnie Moss,

Here are my suggestions for improving student achievement in Hayward Schools.

Smaller class sizes - 30-34 children are too

many

More money for textbooks and library books

More prep time for elementary teachers

In general our schools are doing a good job

Please complete and return to Bonnie Moss.

Dear Bonnie Moss,

Here are my suggestions for improving student achievement in Hayward Schools.

I like your yellow "suggestions" card. I believe in tra-
ditional stuff--the three Rs, plus the arts. Kids who
don't make the grade shouldn't be promoted to the next
grade. Four years ago, I met a young man who'd just
graduated from Tennyson High. He was 98% illiterate.
That's just not acceptable, in any school system.
Save money by streamlining administrative costs. Cut
the fat. Any bureaucracy can survive major surgery.
Encourage creativity, free-thinking, responsibility.
All that kind of stuff. You seem to be well-connected
and a superior fundraiser. You'll probably win--you've
got my vote because you called me one night and we
chatted. Stand up for what's right.

Name (ple

Please complete and return to Bonnie Moss.   10/3

Dear Bonnie Moss,

Here are my suggestions for improving student achievement in Hayward Schools.

I appreciate your concerns
about the neighborhood schools.
I am glad you are taking the
time to visit Haywards School
I support your efforts to gather
ideas for solutions to prevent problems.

Please complete and return to Bonnie Moss.   10/3

Dear Bonnie Moss,

Here are my suggestions for improving student achievement in Hayward Schools.

I agree with every one of your
suggestions - All of them will help, but
only if there is more discipline
at home - they are alone too much at home
while their parents work - consequently they
have no manners toward the adults & the
elderly - Of course all children aren't undisciplined - There are many that are being raised right.
Basically some Teen-agers frighten me -

Name (please print)   Address   Phone

Taking the time to "listen" to people through questionnaires - or asking voters their opinion - makes a candidate's job easier, and they are more likely to be successful.

heard, "Thanks for asking, no one has ever asked me before."

Bonnie kept at her calling every day—35 calls today, 35 calls tomorrow, 35 calls the day after. About a month before the election, when political signs begin to appear like mushrooms after a rain, Bonnie's opponents put up their signs on public property—mainly on telephone poles and in empty lots. Bonnie's signs, by contrast, went up only in the front lawns of real voters, people she had talked to over the last four months. On Election Day, we were able to concentrate on getting only those people she had actually talked to and identified as supporters to vote.

When the votes came in, the election was not even close. Despite being single, with no children in the schools and a relative newcomer to the community, Bonnie was easily elected. Two months later, she began serving her first year of an eight-year career on the Board of Education, during which time she led efforts to fix the schools, helped select a new superintendent and helped settle an acrimonious teachers strike. She also kept up her visits to the schools so she could stay on top of what was going on.

Today, Bonnie is a leading member of my staff, helping school districts, hospital districts and quality candidates. I listen to her as she gives them advice: "To win, you must work harder than you have ever worked before. You must know your community. You must listen to voters *and* you must work hard every day, every damn day."

Bonnie's successful political career began with a simple commitment to make progress every day. The most difficult part was picking up the phone every night and making the first call to a stranger. To do that, she had to overcome her fears.

Chapter Six

Overcome Your Fear

When I first started organizing, I would get sick to my stomach when I had to speak to a group of people. Today, while I am an experienced public speaker, I still get nervous beforehand. It took me years to overcome my fear of speaking publicly, but I have learned that fear is natural, and that it is necessary to overcome your fear if you want to be successful.

Despite over 30 years of experience, every time Election Day approaches, I worry about losing and the impact it will have on my clients and their communities. I know that in each election there will be winners, and there will be losers. I use the fear of losing to motivate myself to work harder and to look for every advantage that will lead to victory.

Risks have to be taken to make change. Being able to take risks, to handle conflict and to overcome fear are essential qualities and without these qualities, it is impossible to win in the public arena.

A healthy political system is dependent on person-to-person contact. Sometimes it is by phone, sometimes door-to-door, sometimes by talking to strangers on a street corner or in a shopping center parking lot.

I have observed people who have been asked to go door-to-door on behalf of a candidate or an issue. Many refuse to do it. They are afraid of rejection. It's not unlike the fourteen-year-old boy standing against the gym wall at his high school dance, too afraid to ask a girl to dance. Fear of rejection is a powerful deterrent—even for adults.

Sometimes fear is personal and irrational, like the fear of speaking publicly or the fear of rejection. But some fear is more than real. The Civil Rights activists of the '50s and '60s, and South Africans fighting against apartheid, were not afraid of rejection. Their fears were about losing their homes, their livelihoods, or even their lives.

Every day of the year, immigrants come to this country looking for a better life. They are often afraid. Many have no money, little education, and few skills, except a willingness to work hard for low pay. My grandfather emigrated from Italy to America at 17. Before he traveled to America, he had never left his small village in Southern Italy. He was afraid to leave his family, afraid of the long trip and what he would face in the new world. He spoke only an Italian dialect and could neither read nor write. He arrived at Ellis Island with only $3.00 in his pocket, the clothes he wore and the name of a distant cousin in Colorado. Like many immigrants before and after him, he struggled and overcame his fear through hard work and courage. He never saw his family again, but he became part of a new American generation of immigrants that built successful lives in their newly adopted country.

Immigrants face hardship and fear every day, but those who are successful are able to overcome their fear, and our country is better for it.

Overcoming fear is one of the key elements to being successful—in life and in politics, and every person who desires to be successful politically has to overcome fear of failure or fear of rejection to be successful.

I learned to overcome my fear in the dusty fields outside Hollister, California.

* * * * *

Burritos at Sunrise

The sun had not risen yet over the mountains east of Hollister. I was looking for groups of farm workers that I could talk to about joining the Union. As I drove up in my battered Nissan truck I could see shadowy silhouettes of about a dozen workers already in the fields, but I could barely make out their figures in the dim morning light.

I got out of the truck, pulling the collar of my jean jacket up to keep the cold wind from blowing down my back. The workers were crouched around a small fire getting warm as they waited for their workday to begin. The foreman (*el majordomo*) had not yet arrived, so I had a few minutes to talk to the workers alone. I had to move quickly. I knew the workers would not talk freely to me in the presence of *el patron* (the "boss"). Fear of losing their jobs if the grower knew they were talking to a union organizer was real.

The Union had recently ended a successful three-week strike against the powerful garlic growers in the Hollister-Gilroy area, who had reluctantly agreed to a 10¢ a bushel increase in piece rate wages. Other growers in the area were worried that workers of other crops would demand more money and better conditions. Tensions were high. The decades old relationships between poor workers and powerful growers were beginning to crumble.

As organizers in the farm workers union, we were eager to build on the success of the strike and take advantage of this momentum. If we could get a majority of the workers to sign union authorization cards we could call for an election. An election would give us the right to negotiate a union contract for better wages and working conditions, but the window for doing this was small, especially since the garlic harvest was now over, and the workers had spread out to work in other crops.

The foreman was due at any time. I had to work fast. But for a moment I hesitated. How was I—a white, middle class, non-farm worker, who spoke Spanish only haltingly—going to convince these workers to join the Union? They would probably laugh at me or worse, just ignore me. I was alone; there was no one to help me. I had two options. I could either do my job and go into the field to talk to the workers, or I could get in my truck and drive away. No one but me would know. I could report I had not found workers, or that I could not get to them. I knew, though, that if I walked away without trying to speak with them, I was finished as an organizer.

I stepped into the field. My fear of failure overcame my fear of rejection.

As I got closer and began to make out the faces of the workers in the dim light, I was disappointed that I did not recognize any of them. It was not going to be easy to get their support since they had no idea who I was.

I approached the fire, walking slowly, cautiously and called out simply, "*Buenos dias, compañeros.*"

The workers looked up, eyeing me but said nothing. It would have been easy to walk away—I almost did. I noticed they were warming burritos wrapped in aluminum foil in the coals of the fire.

I broke the silence by introducing myself in Spanish, "I'm with the United Farm Workers Union," I explained. "The Union is trying to help you get better wages."

One of the workers simply nodded, as he reached out to turn over the burritos in the fire. I continued, directing my question to him, "So did you hear of the wage increase the Union has recently negotiated?"

"*Si,* I heard," he said.

Then, he looked up at me, staring directly into my eyes, as if challenging me or searching for the truth. "So tell me, *Gringo,*" he said, speaking in a mix of Spanish and English, "why is a non-farm worker up so early in the morning (*La Madrugada*) to talk to us?"

"Because I've been working with Cesar Chavez, and I thought you'd be interested in hearing about the Union," I said. "Are you happy with what you're paid? Do you ever get sick and need medical care? Aren't you tired of the boss pushing you around?" I asked the questions one after another.

I felt the eyes of the workers watching me closely. Then, one of the men sitting next to the worker turning the burritos asked me if I was hungry, "*Tienes hambre joven?*"

"Yes, I am," I said, and the worker who had called me "*Gringo*" handed me a hot burrito of egg, potato and green chili. The first rays of dawn began spreading through the valley, but the air was still cold, and I pulled my jacket close as we ate.

Speaking in Spanish, one of the workers told me, "My cousin is a *Chavista.*" (The term the farm workers use to refer to Union activists loyal to Cesar Chavez.) As we ate, I handed out union cards and explained that I needed the workers to sign the cards and get others to sign them also to show they supported the union.

Then, as the sun rose slowly over the mountains, the foreman pulled up in his pickup truck.

"You must go now," said one of the workers as he motioned towards the foreman, indicating the workday was about to begin.

"I'll sign your card," he added, "and I'll get the others to sign them, too. I'll bring them to the union office."

I smiled and shook his hand and then left. I had accomplished my mission.

My fears had evaporated with the morning dew, and I learned something about myself that morning—overcoming your fear begins with taking a step forward.

* * * * *

As an organizer, I often have to try to get people to do something they do not, at first, want to do. Sometimes I am successful, sometimes I am not. Some people are afraid of conflict. Some are fearful of the work involved and some fear failure. One method of teaching people how to overcome fear is to tell them stories of how others have done it. Several years ago, I tried to persuade a parent to run for a seat on her local Board of Education. She was bright, articulate, cared about children, had a background in finance, taught school years before and was well respected by all who knew her. She was an ideal candidate except for one flaw—she was afraid.

"I'd just melt if people yelled at me," she said. "I hate conflict. I don't know what I'd do if I had to choose between what teachers wanted and what parents wanted. I'm afraid, Larry."

I told her, "Frances, (not her real name) the fear you have is real, and I respect you for telling me. But it is nothing compared to the fear a child has on their first day of school when she doesn't speak English, or the fear someone has of losing a job or their home."

Then I told her, "Listen, I have a story about fear and how some people overcame their fear. These people didn't want conflict either, but they knew that if they didn't overcome their fears, they would lose their homes. After you've heard this story, you tell me whether you think you can overcome your own fears and do the right thing."

My story was about how farm workers, in danger of losing their homes, stood together and accomplished a miracle. Despite huge odds, by overcoming their fears, they won a momentous victory. This is their story:

We will not be Moved

I had just been assigned to be the director of a United Farm Workers field office in Oxnard, California, near Ventura on the California coast. At about 9:30 one morning, I got a frantic call from Maria Elena, a *campesina* who lived in Cabrillo Village—a farm labor camp on the outskirts of Oxnard.

The camp, which housed families, was in better shape than many of the deplorable labor camps that served as temporary housing for farm workers. Many of the houses in the camp were simple, small, wood-framed homes where farm workers and their children lived. While the camp was owned by citrus growers, the farm workers who lived in the camp were some of the strongest pro-UFW workers in California. The workers had recently voted under California's new Agricultural Relations Law to be represented by the UFW. Negotiations had not started yet, and it was not clear whether a contract could be negotiated. The citrus harvest was ending and some of the workers were packing up to move north with the harvest. To intimidate the remaining workers, and to make sure no pro-UFW workers moved back into the camp, every time a family moved out of a house, the company ordered the house destroyed.

Maria Elena was in tears as she described what was happening. Next door to her a bulldozer was approaching a house that had just been vacated by a family moving north. The driver had been instructed to demolish the simple, wooden-frame building.

"What do we do? What do we do?" she screamed into the phone. I had only been "in charge" of the local UFW field office for a few weeks and this crisis demanded someone with more experience than I had. *What would Cesar do?* I thought.

"Surround the house," I yelled over the phone. "Get every child, every person in the camp to surround the house. You must stop the bulldozer. I'll be there as quickly as I can."

Maria Elena pushed back her tears, strengthened now by a plan, albeit temporarily. "Yes, I'll do that. Right away."

Maria Elena hung up the phone and raced from house to house alerting everyone in the camp to join together around the threatened house. I tried to reach Cesar to tell him about the looming crisis and to ask him for direction and advice. I called Esther Winterrowd, his secretary, to say that I needed to speak with Cesar immediately about a crisis that needed his attention. I found he was at a meeting in Calexico, near the Mexican border, about six hours away. Unfortunately, in those days, before cell phones and pagers, I could not contact him directly myself. I had to depend on him getting the message from others and then calling me.

"I'm going out to the camp right now, but I'll be back at my house later tonight," I told her. "Please have him call me!"

Then, I headed to the labor camp. When I arrived, about twenty minutes later, the women and children in the camp, alerted by Maria Elena, had completely surrounded the house and were singing, "*No nos moveran*" (we will not be moved). There were only a few men there, most were either too old to be picking lemons or were injured.

Just beyond them, the bulldozer driver was sitting in the cab of his massive, yellow machine, facing the group and looking bewildered, unsure what to do now. As I approached him, he called out to me, "Hey, man, I don't want no trouble. I don't want to do this."

Meanwhile, just as I began speaking to the driver, the foreman of the

Larry Tramutola and fellow UFW organizer, Ken Fijimoto, confer at Cabrillo Village, near Oxnard, California, about organizing support to save farm workers' houses from being demolished.

camp drove up in his new pickup truck, followed by two police cars. The foreman jumped out of his truck, his face like a bright red overripe beet, and he marched towards the women.

He spoke angrily, yelling at them. Waving his arms, he screamed, "Get away from that house! You have no right to be here!"

But the women and the children, joined by the few men, did not move. They just stared back at him, and he turned to the police, telling them to force the farm workers to move. The police officer in charge conferred briefly with the other officers, called police headquarters on his walkie-talkie, and then, to our shock, told the foreman, no, they would do nothing. They would stay there in the event of any violence, but otherwise, they would do nothing. As the officer told him, "This is the farm workers' camp, and they're not trespassing. So they have a right to stand there, and we can't do anything."

We were deadlocked—the farm worker women and children singing, the foreman ranting, the police standing by observing. A woman went up to the bulldozer driver and said to him, "What is your name? Do you have children? Do you have a home? You're a worker just like us. How could you do this? Why don't you just leave?" She then quietly stared at him, not saying anything and not moving from in front of the bulldozer.

Finally, after about 20 minutes of intense standoff, the bulldozer driver started the engine and drove away, telling the foreman, "I've got other things to do. I don't want any part of this." As he drove off, a cheer erupted among the workers. We had won, at least temporarily. Angrily, the foreman turned and stormed off back to his truck and drove off in a cloud of dust. Everybody yelled. *Si se puede!* It can be done! There were tears of joy as well as a real concern about what we were going to do next.

That night I spoke to Cesar on the phone.

"I'll drive to the camp and meet with the workers tomorrow night," he said. "You just get them there, and then we'll discuss what to do."

The next day when Cesar arrived, everyone was at the meeting in force—about 200 people. We gathered in the yard outside one of the homes—men, women and children—some standing, some sitting on the grass. Maria Elena and a few other workers told Cesar what had happened the previous day. Cesar listened, then responded quietly suggesting, "Perhaps you should buy the camp."

"Buy the camp!?"

I was astonished. Surely the idea was impossible since the workers had so few resources. They were barely surviving from day to day on the meager wages they earned. How could they consider buying the whole camp? But I kept these thoughts to myself and said nothing.

Cesar said he would meet with small groups of the workers, and one of the families volunteered their home for Cesar to use. That evening I watched in stunned silence as groups of workers, ten to fifteen at a time, came inside to meet with him. He told stories about what other workers in other places had been able to accomplish by working together. Mostly, he spoke about overcoming fear. He told them, "Your biggest problem is your own fear, and unless you make a commitment to yourselves and your families to fight, you will always be kicked out of somewhere. You need to take a stand, if not now, then someday, when you finally overcome your fear." Clearly, Cesar thought that this was the time to make a stand, but he did not tell the workers what to do. It was up to them to make their own decisions.

Cesar persuaded not by fancy rhetoric or impassioned speeches. Instead, he looked people in their eyes as he spoke softly and clearly. He also made them laugh, and the laughter helped everyone overcome their fear. I am sure many of them had doubts whether or not they would be successful, but Cesar had succeeded in helping them put aside their fears and take a stand.

By the time the meetings ended, very late at night, Cesar had talked to every family in the camp. Only a few families chose to move out. Most decided they would do whatever was necessary to save the camp and the houses.

Having made this decision and committed themselves to this goal, they then needed to create a plan that would get them there. The first step was to form a committee to meet with the growers who owned the camp. Another group was to travel to Sacramento to investigate the possibility of state funding, and another group was assigned to meet with Union attorneys to obtain an injunction to stop more homes from being destroyed. Finally, the workers began planning a campaign to raise funds.

Over the next few months, the committee mobilized, the lawyers filed their suit, and the workers gathered funds to support their efforts. Three years later, the workers achieved their goal. They obtained a state grant, which set aside funds to allow them to purchase the camp and develop a community housing cooperative. By mastering their fears, they had mastered their fate, and it all started with a few workers taking a stand.

Postscript

Ten years later, the power of their accomplishment dramatically came home to me when I was giving a talk on organizing at Stanford University. A young student came up to me when I had finished and said he remembered me. He told me he was the son of one of the migrant farm workers who had met with Cesar and me that night. He and his mother were two of the people who had surrounded the house.

"My family decided to stay and fight," he told me. "Our home at the labor camp was the first permanent home we ever had, and that made it possible for me to attend the local schools and the local community college. Then, I eventually transferred to Stanford, and I have just been accepted to law school. Cesar changed my life that night. I will always be grateful to him for what he did."

* * * * *

"Frances," whom I had attempted to convince to run for office, decided not to. While she had many of the attributes needed to be a successful school board member, she lacked the most important one—courage. Courage, like discipline, is developed not by leaping forward but by taking small steps. Frances was unwilling to take a small step because of her fear of being criticized. It takes courage to take a stand, whether it is fighting to save your home or disagreeing with popular sentiment. Francis would never know what she was capable of achieving.

All successful people have fears they overcame: fear of failure, fear of speaking, fear of being yelled at, fear of being ignored, fear of financial loss, fear of rejection. Cesar Chavez, Fred Ross Sr. and many of the great organizers I have worked with over the years taught me important lessons about overcoming fear. Among the most important are these:

Fear is natural. You can either let it paralyze you, or you can use it to motivate yourself.

Successful people are those who recognize their fears and take appropriate steps to overcome them. Speaking publicly, debating and going door-to-door to talk to people are skills learned through trying. When Cesar was a young organizer trying to organize house meetings, he drove around the block several times before pulling together enough courage to go into the house to talk to people. Overcoming his shyness and fear was his first step in becoming an organizer.

Cesar taught us many lessons about organizing people. One of the most valuable was to be color-blind dealing with people. A good organizer is able to organize people regardless of their race. Fred Ross organized Mexican-Americans without speaking a word of Spanish. Cesar's cousin, Manuel, organized workers in Florida who were primarily African-American. Farm workers who spoke only Spanish were sent to the cities across the U.S. and Canada to built support for their Union.

Laughter has great power to dispel fear.

Laughter helps people relax. By telling stories that made people laugh, Cesar was able to help workers who were afraid of losing their homes and their jobs overcome their fears. When I began training organizers, I videotaped their presentations. Replaying the tapes were often great sources of amusement and laughter as we poked fun at ourselves. Every campaign should look for opportunities for fun. While work is serious, do not take yourself so seriously that you cannot enjoy the process.

Overcoming fear is an ongoing process. Do not force it.

Although I still get "butterflies" before speaking publicly, I have learned how to channel my nervousness. Years ago, I had to stand in for Cesar, who was unable to speak to a group of church leaders in Palo Alto. I was utterly afraid. I was afraid of doing poorly. I was afraid that I would make a fool of myself. I was afraid of failing. I did not want to speak, and I tried every excuse to get out of speaking. Dolores Huerta, Cesar's long-time colleague and co-founder of the UFW, brought me down to earth with her wisdom. She said, "Larry, if you do a poor job, no one will remember; if you do a great job, no one will remember. But if you don't do it, the next time will be harder for *you*. Do it. Do your best and learn from the experience."

Do not show your fear to others.

That is what the farm workers did when they put aside their fears to stand in the face of the bulldozers. Some were nervous and shaking inside, but they did not show it. Instead, by standing united around the house and refusing to move, they showed strength—not fear. Perception is reality. Act strong and confident, and others will perceive and respond to you that way.

The most important fear to overcome is the fear of failing.

The only people who fail are those who never try. Most successful elected officials have lost elections during their careers. Most athletes lose. A *great* baseball player fails to get a hit 2 out of every 3 times at bat. If you want to make a difference (and isn't that the only reason to be involved in politics?), *expect conflict and the possibility of losing.*

Chapter Seven

Develop the Will to Win

One of the most remarkable commercials on late night cable TV (before it was removed from the airways for deceptive advertising) was for "Exercise in a Bottle." The spokesperson, a former major league baseball player, claimed that a person could eat whatever they wanted including hamburgers, french fries, thick creamy chocolate shakes and fried food, but *if* they took the pills in "Exercise in a Bottle," the pills would absorb the fat and calories, and the person would not gain weight.

Despite the ludicrous claims, thousands of people—looking for easy, effortless results—purchased "Exercise in a Bottle" hoping they could indeed become fit without effort.

Success in politics, like being in top physical condition, is a result of effort over time, and there are no easy steps. Successful candidates, more often than not, are those who put in greater effort than their opponents. In local elections, that is almost always the case.

Losing weight is possible if you are able to develop a step-by-step plan for achieving success. It starts with setting a goal and then developing habits for achieving good health. Reaching the goal takes effort and consistency over an extended period of time. Likewise, political success is a result of being able to clearly articulate what you want to accomplish, breaking down that goal into smaller achievable steps and then completing those steps. People who have the discipline to do that have a significant advantage over their opposition. I have worked with clients who had a vision of what they wanted, and they developed and followed a plan to achieve their vision. I have also worked with clients who had a vision for what they wanted but were clueless when it came to understanding how to achieve their goal.

Successful politicians and organizers are able to articulate a clear vision of what they want to achieve and then develop a step-by-step plan to produce the results they desire.

What are the steps to achieving success?

Step One: Articulate your goal and the steps you need to take to reach it.

What is your goal? Is it winning an election? Organizing a union? Stopping a bad development project? Losing 20 pounds? What do you need to do to achieve that goal?

Prior to Senator Barbara Boxer's successful run for U.S. Senate, my wife, Ann, and I were invited to spend the weekend at an isolated bed and breakfast in Northern California with Barbara, her husband, Stuart, Congressman George Miller, various friends of Barbara and several other "political insiders" to discuss Barbara's political future. Surrounded by oak trees and the golden hills of Sonoma County, we pontificated on how difficult (and unwise) it would be for Barbara to give up her safe Congressional seat, and the growing power and seniority she was gaining in Congress, in order to make an almost certainly unsuccessful try for the Senate. We talked about the money it would take and the fact that Barbara had little "name recognition" outside of her congressional district.

Barbara listened and said, "Today, there is just one woman in the entire U.S. Senate. That's intolerable. I want to be in the Senate! I don't care if I have to give up my seat in Congress. I want to be in the Senate!"

She did not worry about her potential opposition, her lack of statewide name recognition, the amount of money she would need to raise or the seemingly insurmountable odds against her winning. Barbara's goal was to be in the Senate.

"I would rather lose than not make the effort," she said. That was it. End of discussion. The decision was made. The vision was clear—Senate or nothing. To achieve that goal, Barbara and her supporters made a plan to visit every community in the state that she could visit. She would focus on women voters in the Democratic primary since she was the only woman in the crowded field. She would devote all of her time to campaigning and to raising the needed funds—she would encourage thousands of small donors, primarily women, to support her efforts.

One year later, when Barbara was sworn in as California's junior Senator, I asked her what the key was to her winning. She said, "I believed in myself, and I believed that we were on the side of history. More importantly though, we had a goal and we just worked like hell."

Step Two: Develop the discipline to succeed.

Most people want to succeed. Most want to be healthy. Success and health are usually the result of successful habits practiced on a regular and consistent basis. Successful people usually have developed a work ethic that allows them to achieve their goals. In this sense, successful politicians are like successful athletes.

John Wooden, the Hall of Fame basketball coach at UCLA, declared, "There is no substitute for work. Worthwhile results come from hard work and careful planning." His contemporary, Fred Ross, Sr. taught organizers to be accountable for every minute of their 24 hour day, from rest to eating to meeting with people. His goal was to instill personal discipline in every organizer so that good habits became part of a daily routine.

Step Three: Enjoy what you do.

Quincy Jones, the great American composer and musician, told a group of Harvard graduates that success comes from doing what you love. Jones recalled in his speech that years ago, he and four friends, all struggling young artists, stood outside the door of the Birdland nightclub in New York. Between them they could not scrape together enough money to hear Charlie Parker perform. Fame and fortune was a long way away. Among them was a young Italian-American kid, an aspiring thespian from Omaha, Nebraska, who had just landed his first role in a Broadway play—Marlon Brando. Another one was a Jamaican folk singer who could not get a gig, poor as hell and stuck with a penchant for Calypso music—Harry Belafonte. The fourth was from the Bahamas, an unemployed actor with a deep voice and full of great presence, who had been turned down for one acting job after another and was now waiting on tables to make ends meet—Sydney Poitier.

These four friends stood outside in the cold with not a penny between them listening to the music through the door of the night club. No one knew at the time that they would win Academy Awards, Grammies and become wealthier than they could have ever imagined. They all became successful because they had passion, and they did what they loved. Jones challenged the students not to work for money but to follow their dreams, and through hard work and love, success will come.

Sacrifice is overrated. Anybody who is great at anything usually loves what he or she is doing. Tiger Woods loves the game of golf. While he loves to win, he practices harder and longer than his competitors. The successful clients I have worked with over the years, whether elected officials, superintendents of schools, union leaders or business leaders, all enjoyed what they were doing and they all enjoyed putting in the extra effort that allowed them to be successful.

To put in the effort to accomplish great things, you have to love to do the work. If you do not, you will look for short cuts and excuses to get out of doing the work. Successful campaigners work late into the evenings and weekends, not because they have to but because they want to.

Step Four: Push yourself out of your comfort zone.

Improving physical stamina involves pushing your body incrementally harder. To gain strength or improve endurance, you need to push yourself past your previous limits. Elections are won by reaching out beyond your base of supporters and communicating to people who may not share your vision or goals. For example, school tax elections cannot be won if the campaign does not persuade people who do not have children in public schools. Minority candidates must often reach out to nonethnic voters. Public hospitals, needing voter support to rebuild aging facilities need support from those who may never need their services.

Campaign workers are often afraid to reach out across racial lines. Insurance companies illegally "red line" certain communities, charging higher insurance rates to people living in poorer neighborhoods. Campaigns do not call it red lining, but they participate in the same form of discrimination. Campaign workers are routinely cautioned to avoid walking door-to-door in certain areas.

I have walked hundreds of precincts and knocked on thousands of doors. I have found that minority voters are no different from anybody else. Some will talk, others will not. Some are nice, others are rude. To be successful, you must push yourself out of familiar surroundings, and if you want to win, you need to push yourself out of your comfort zone.

* * * * *

Matt Muckler is a state representative in Missouri. Matt is white and represents a district that is more than 60% African-American. When he first ran for office in the Democratic primary, his opponent was the son of the incumbent, a popular African-American elected official, and who was the odds on favorite to win. Matt's opponent had the endorsement of organized labor, the congressman, other elected officials and some Democratic clubs.

During the summer months before Missouri's primary, the weather in St. Louis can be described as sweltering. Matt walked (and sweated) every day through the months of May, June and July. He walked every door and talked to every voter. He introduced himself at front doors and listened to voters' concerns.

His opponent did not walk in the neighborhoods and, instead, went to endorsement meetings and plastered public thoroughfares with signs and voters' homes with mail.

On Election Day, Matt won with 56% of the vote. He won with the support of black voters who he had met going door-to-door in their community. He won because he was willing to work outside of his "comfort zone" and talk to people about real issues.

Step Five: Be willing to take risks.

Jerry Davis recently retired as the superintendent of schools in Manhattan Beach, California. The Manhattan Beach School District is one of California's most successful public school districts with high test scores, motivated students and great teachers and principals. Being the superintendent of schools in Manhattan Beach could be considered a plum job. The district is well-managed and well-regarded. It would be seemingly easy to manage a district that appears to run so well; however, the reason Manhattan Beach schools are so successful is that Jerry Davis has a quality that is too rare among school superintendents.

Jerry Davis is not afraid to take risks. Three times in five years Jerry asked the community to support tax increases, all requiring 66.7% approval, to improve the schools (two elections were to improve facilities and one to improve programs). Despite opposition from fiscal conservatives and those who feared losing, Jerry continually has taken the position that: My job is to take risks. If we don't stick our necks out we won't make progress. Although not an elected official, Jerry has the will to win. He is not afraid to fail. As he says "Failing is not taking risks."

While many people "want to win," the winners have a burning desire and the discipline to make the sacrifices necessary to win. If you do not have the passion to win you will not be very good in politics or organizing.

To succeed in politics or community organizing, you have to eat, sleep and breathe winning. Elections are not about "running a good campaign" or "raising issues." They are about winning. In every election, someone wins and someone loses. Ask a football fan who was the losing team in the last Super Bowl and they'd be hard pressed to tell you. Few can remember who the second place team is in any sport. Sports and politics revolve around *winning*. Some people have it, others don't.

* * * * *

During the presidential campaign in 1988, I had been chosen along with Bob Lawson, a skilled and veteran organizer, to direct the California field operation for the Democratic Party. Our mission was to conduct a voter registration effort in California and to increase voter turnout in heavily Democratic areas. These efforts were designed to help Michael Dukakis win the Presidency.

Any college freshman political science student knows that to win the Presidency, the Democratic nominee has to win California. (Only one Democratic nominee for President had won California since Truman won in 1948). We knew that to win California we had to increase turnout in the vote-rich, turnout-light minority communities of Los Angeles and the Bay Area. (At the time, we had no idea that Dukakis would suffer a devastating defeat and that he would win barely 100 electoral votes). We were extremely concerned that if Democratic voter turnout was low, it would affect not only the Presidential campaign but also the campaigns of hundreds of Democratic candidates who were in tight races up and down the state.

We had set up campaign offices in 103 mostly minority communities from San Ysidro on the Mexican border to Crescent City near Oregon over 1000 miles away. Thousands of Democrats, tired of the anti-environmental, anti-labor, anti-choice policies of the Reagan/Bush administration, were eager to become volunteers.

Our campaign focused on "less likely voters." Over 400,000 of these voters were targeted for special attention, as we knew we needed their votes to win. But in every minority community from Oakland to South Central LA to San Diego, we heard the same thing: Why doesn't Dukakis come into our communities, visit our churches, and meet with us? Does he not respect us? Does he not want to be seen surrounded by blacks or Hispanics?

We had heard it many times.

About two months were left until Election Day. We knew that to increase turnout we needed to inject some life into our efforts in the minority neighborhoods, and we needed to convince Dukakis himself to come into the communities we were organizing. We needed him to attend Get Out the Vote rallies in the minority communities and give people a reason for voting.

The "national campaign" was focused on making Governor Dukakis appealing to white middle class voters, and press coverage showing the governor speaking to a crowd of black or Hispanic voters was not the image the national campaign wanted. Leading in the polls, Dukakis and his advisors were not eager to change their strategy.

For weeks, we had lobbied Tony Podesta, Dukakis' California director and brother of John Podesta (who later became President Clinton's Chief of Staff) to allow us a chance to sit down with Dukakis. Podesta supported our efforts but was too distracted by the pressures of raising money, keeping the national campaign happy and satisfying the needs of Democratic office holders up and down the state to lobby hard for us. Podesta was not from California, and like most "East Coast" consultants who come into California for campaigns, his view of the Golden State was acquired from five star hotels in San Francisco or plush homes in West Los Angeles.

As Election Day neared, concerns were increasing that Dukakis' once huge lead was slipping and that Democrats could lose both the State Assembly and Senate if turnout was not increased. On Saturday September 2, 1988, Dukakis was scheduled to give an environmental address at Crissy Field on the San Francisco Bay, with the Golden Gate Bridge and Golden Gate Recreation Area as the perfect back drop for the 11:00 news. Late on Friday, the day before, Lawson and I learned that Podesta had set up our meeting with Dukakis, and we would be allowed to travel in his limousine as his motorcade traveled from Crissy Field to the San Francisco International Airport.

Bob and I arrived at Crissy Field armed with facts and statistics—the number of volunteers we had recruited, the number of voters we needed to get to vote. We were given VIP security passes, and after Dukakis' speech, we were ushered into the Governor's limousine.

I had never been in a presidential motorcade before, much less in a limousine with the Democratic nominee for President of the United States. We rode through the empty streets of San Francisco, down the Bayshore Freeway, eerily absent of traffic thanks to our Secret Service motorcade escort. We had 20 minutes to convince Michael Dukakis that his campaign in California was doomed unless he and his team spent some time and effort in the minority communities.

As we rode, we told him that people were concerned that he had not visited the minority Hispanic and African-American communities, and that if he did, we were confident we could inspire people to vote. We encouraged him to schedule time to visit the minority communities. To bring the point home, we told him stories of people who had registered for the very first time and that people wanted a reason to vote. We told him that many voters were sons and daughters of immigrants who did not have traditions of voting.

We could have been talking to a wall. He was polite and he nodded appropriately at times. When we said "immigrant" he went into his often repeated, "I can't believe that I, the son of a Greek immigrant, have received the nomination of President." Bob and I held our tongues although we both wanted to scream, "The goal is to BE President, not to be NOMINATED!"

We wanted to tell him that sometimes campaigns are about the candidate, but they are also about the issues that are raised, the people who are activated, the communities that are touched. A candidate has a responsibility to more than just himself. Low voter turnout is often due to uninspiring candidates and campaigns that do not reach out to voters.

Maybe Dukakis knew at that time that he had no chance of winning, or maybe he had bought into the conventional strategy that he had to appeal to the political middle.

When we arrived at the San Francisco Airport, Governor Dukakis thanked us for our perspective and said he would do what he could. The governor was off to another photo op in Southern California. Bob and I got out of the limo and looked at each other. We tossed our VIP badges into a nearby trash can. Michael Dukakis was evidently not interested in taking risks, at least not yet. He was still up in the polls. It would take a few weeks before his managers would realize he could not win without the support of minority voters. We knew that by then, it would be too late. Michael Dukakis lacked one very important quality—the will to win.

Cesar Chavez: The Will to Win

La Paz, the United Farm Workers headquarters, is located in the Tehachapi Mountains, about 30 miles east of Bakersfield. Formerly a tuberculosis sanitarium, it served as the home to Cesar Chavez, his family and much of the UFW staff. The isolated location of La Paz served three purposes. First, it provided Cesar and the top leadership of the Union a place for reflection, study and debate without phone interruptions and other distractions. Second, it provided Cesar with a higher level of security than was possible in other less remote areas. Threats to Cesar were a real concern in the '60s and '70s. (Both Cesar's friend, Robert F. Kennedy, and his contemporary, Martin Luther King, Jr. had recently been assassinated.). Third, it removed Cesar from the adoring crowds of farm workers and farm worker supporters and allowed the farm workers themselves to develop their own leadership skills without Cesar being constantly present.

There were downsides as well. The staff was isolated physically from the UFW membership, living conditions were spartan and recreational facilities and outside activities virtually non-existent.

After six years working in various UFW offices from Florida to California, I was asked by Cesar to work out of La Paz and coordinate the activities of various union offices and staff around the country.

Often during the summer months, when the heat was well over 100 degrees during the day, Cesar would invite five or six of us to go to Bakersfield late in the evening to play handball at the outdoor courts. By this time of the day, the heat had lessened and the crowds of onlookers who regularly appeared if Cesar was present wouldn't be around.

We would leave La Paz at about 10 P.M. and return at 1-2 in the morning. I welcomed the chance to go. It was an opportunity to drive 30- 40 minutes with Cesar and get his advice on projects I was working on. He was always more relaxed in these settings and willing to share advice and frustrations.

The handball games were spirited. We played doubles and singles, depending on who came and the level of competition. Cesar always wanted to be matched up against the best person in singles and with the best in doubles. Losing was not something he did easily or willingly. Sometimes I was matched with him, sometimes against. Every questionable point was challenged. Every debatable call went his way. He made himself both player and referee. If we were playing the best of three and he lost, it would become the best of five. If we were playing to 15 points and he was on the short end, the game would be extended to 21. I learned a lot playing these games with Cesar. At his core, he was competitive. He wanted—he needed—to win. What ever he did, he wanted to be the best.

Much of what has been written about Cesar Chavez suggests that Cesar was larger than life, a heroic figure, devoted to nonviolent struggle. While there is an element of truth in those descriptions, those of us who worked in the UFW know there were other aspects of Cesar that were rarely appreciated.

As a young organizer, I was amazed at the physical and mental punishment Cesar Chavez was able to inflict upon himself and the discipline he had to keep going. He worked 17-20 hour days, often driving in the middle of the night to make a meeting the next day. He constantly read about other labor and political leaders and social movements and was usually the first to work in the morning and the last to leave at night. Cesar worked harder than others who were half his age.

Cesar, like great athletes, had an ability to focus his mind and his body on winning. He was able to visualize what it would feel like to win and to articulate that vision to his staff, to farm workers and to the public. This ability to totally focus on winning and making the sacrifices necessary to win allowed Cesar to achieve success when many others before him had failed. We normally associate the will to win with athletes who push their bodies to the point of exhaustion in an attempt to gain a winning edge. Cesar Chavez was as competitive as any world class athlete. Most successful leaders are as well.

In our many conversations after playing, Cesar and I discussed the attributes of winning and what it took to be able to win. We often discussed winning in terms of athletic competition, but the same lessons are true in politics and community organizing. Here are some of the lessons about winning that I learned from Cesar:

Winners have the commitment to make the sacrifices necessary to achieve their goals. Success comes from working harder than the opposition. It often means working evenings and weekends—there are no shortcuts. The unfortunate downside of this is that winners, be they athletes or organizers or elected officials, are rarely people that have the most balanced personal lives.

As a young organizer, I was amazed at the physical and mental punishment Cesar Chavez was able to inflict upon himself and the discipline he had to keep going. He worked 17-20 hour days, often driving in the middle of the night to make a meeting the next day. He constantly read about other labor and political leaders and social movements and was usually the first to work in the morning and the last to leave at night. Cesar worked harder than others who were half his age.

Balancing personal life with professional responsibilities takes effort.

Winners are able to reevaluate their goals and plans midstream, and make adjustments if something is not working. It is not always possible to put out the best performance. Successful major league pitchers learn how to win when they do not have their "best stuff." Winning is a process of adjustments, modifications, reacting and learning from experience. (Michael Dukakis lacked the ability to respond to attacks midstream. His campaign developed its game plan then kept on it, even when it was not working).

Winners are able to delegate responsibility. Winning is usually a result of teamwork. Even world class athletes involved in individual competitions rely on others. Being able to delegate and bring out the best in others is essential to winning in any endeavor. Teamwork and cooperation are essential qualities.

Winners are able to visualize what it would feel like to lose. For Cesar, it was not hard to visualize what losing would mean. For farm workers, it meant more poverty, terrible working conditions, no control over pesticides, children caught in a web of poverty. Losing wasn't an option.

Winners have the ability to work hard even when the spotlight is not on. Long after the press had moved on to other stories and the struggle of farm workers was out of the limelight, Cesar kept working. He had little desire for press attention or personal recognition. The best athletes exhibit the same commitment. Tiger Woods hits hundreds of golf shots before most of his competitors are out of bed. Campaigns are won by burning the late night oil, preparing and looking for an advantage. John Wooden, the legendary basketball coach who won 11 national championships at UCLA, preached the importance of practicing perfectly. Good habits lead to successful performance.

Winners allow others to share in the victory. Cesar was always gracious to acknowledge the contributions of others. Farm workers were the heroes, not Cesar. At every meeting, reports were given of the sacrifices and success of others who had contributed to the effort. In many ways, he was embarrassed by the attention given to him. The true winner recognizes others are part of his success and makes an effort to acknowledge them and their contribution.

Winners are able to turn defeats into victories. Cesar always tried to create situations where even a loss was turned into a victory. Whether an election or a campaign was won or lost, the campaign provided an opportunity to organize people and to gain new converts to the cause.

Winners also know how to lose. They do not like it. They try to avoid it at all costs. But if they do lose, they are gracious in acknowledging their opponents' victory. Only by respecting an opponent can a person learn what he needs to do to win the next time. In my own career, I have found that I hate losing more than I enjoy winning, but I try to recognize the efforts of my opponents and congratulate them, even if it pains me to do so.

Finally, winners follow a plan for winning. They do not rely on luck, good fortune or the ineptitude of their opponents. They figure out how to win and follow the steps to success.

SIDEWALK STRATEGY #3

FIGURE OUT HOW TO WIN

In 1787, Thomas Jefferson said, "We in America do not have government by the majority; we have government by the majority who participate." Today, over 200 years later—despite a lower voting age; legal protections to all citizens regardless of gender, race or ethnic origin; election materials in numerous languages; the ability to vote by mail or over extended periods—voting participation is at an all time low.

Who is elected to represent us and what ballot measures pass or fail is being decided by fewer and fewer people. As fewer people vote, the influence and importance of those who do vote increases.

Sidewalk Strategy #1 is "Work for what you believe in." Strategy #2 discussed developing the discipline to win. Knowing what you believe in and developing the discipline to win are important, but to get people to vote for you or your cause, you need to figure out *how to win*—Sidewalk Strategy #3.

Winning elections is not unlike winning a sporting event. To win, you need to know the rules of the game, and you need to know what constitutes a win. In football, the winner is not the team that gains the most yardage or holds the ball longer or plays better, it is the team that scores the most points. The winning team rarely wins through luck but by being better prepared and effectively utilizing the talents of each member of the team. Likewise, in politics, the winner is not who runs the best campaign or who is the better candidate but who gets the most votes.

The starting point for knowing how to win, and the subject of Chapter Eight, is to understand how many votes you need to win.

Effectively managing people, money and time are as important in politics as they are in business. Chapter Nine discusses how to develop a clear and specific campaign plan that effectively utilizes all three.

Chapter Ten is about using time to your advantage. Time is a precious resource, and it is the easiest resource to waste. Self-organization is the key to managing time. An organizer can not afford to waste an hour or a day. Every day should start with a plan of what you want to accomplish, and a campaign uses every day successfully.

The final chapter, Chapter Eleven, under Sidewalk Strategy #3 is perhaps the most important: understanding the importance of one single vote and the effort it takes to get one person to vote. This chapter talks about how to motivate people to vote and how to develop the skills and organization to get people to vote.

Chapter Eight

How Many Votes Do You Need?

Campaigns for local offices and local ballot measures generally have limited financial resources, so it is important to spend those limited resources on the voters most likely to participate in the election. Every campaign should begin with an analysis of who is likely to vote in a specific election and an estimate of the number of votes necessary to win. Money and effort spent on people who will not vote is money and effort wasted.

Once you have a clear idea of how many votes it will take to win, you are well on your way to winning. This most basic and important step is often forgotten as candidates and campaigns get caught up designing stylish brochures, developing broad strategy and preparing for debates and interviews. Precious little time is spent determining how many votes are needed to win and where those votes will come from. Without this analysis, it is unlikely that campaign resources will be spent properly and your chances of winning will be significantly diminished.

We grow up playing all kinds of competitive games where the object is to beat your opponent—usually one point more than your opponent is enough. As in sports, if you ask most people how many votes are needed to win an election, they will probably say one more than your opponent. Often, that is not the case. Determining what constitutes a win in an election can be much more complex than that. Here are three examples:

In California, passing a local school tax may require obtaining 55% or 66.7% of the vote, it depends on the election date, the amount of the tax, the type of tax and what else is on the ballot. If the measure requires a special election, you will need 66.7%. If it is a bond measure and there are other issues on the ballot, a mere 55% will get you the win. But while you need 55% or 66.7% of the vote to pass local school bonds, you need only a simple majority (50% +1) for statewide school bonds. Local school bonds can be passed at 55% approval. Local school parcel taxes 66.7%, state school bonds at 50%+1. Confusing? You bet!

In national elections, what counts is winning the majority of electoral college votes, not winning the popular votes. Al Gore lost the presidency in 2000, even though he received almost a million more votes than George W. Bush. That is because the only votes that really counted in that election were the electoral college votes.

Some elections require a simple majority, some a plurality. It is possible that if there are numerous candidates running for the same seat, the winner might win with 20% of the vote or less.

Calculating how many votes you need to win is the first step to winning. Every campaign should start with a campaign plan, and every campaign plan should begin with an analysis of how many votes are needed to win.

In April 2002, we convinced voters in a midsized California city to approve a tax to benefit a community hospital. Before we contacted one voter or wrote one piece of mail, we analyzed the number of people likely to vote in a special election. We studied voter turnout in past elections in this community and estimated what it might be in this election. We then multiplied that number by 66.7% to determine the minimum number of votes we needed to win (the tax required two-thirds approval). Our analysis revealed that approximately 13,450 of the 37,000 registered voters in the community would be likely to vote in the coming election. From previous experience, we knew that about 20% of the people who we would identify as supporters would not actually vote—based on hundreds of previous elections that we had managed where we learned that at least one in five voters who *say* they will vote when asked, do not actually vote. We therefore determined that we would need to find approximately 11,000 people who would commit to vote "yes." This is the formula we used:

13,450 (registered voters who we determined were likely to vote)
X .667 (the percent we needed to win)
8,971 (the number of votes we estimated we needed to win)
+1,900 (people who would "say" they'd vote yes, but wouldn't vote)
10,871 (minimum number of people we needed to identify as supporters)

We then conducted a poll of likely voters to determine the existing level of support for the bond. The results were discouraging. If only *likely* voters voted, there was no chance we could win. To be successful, it would be absolutely essential to find supporters among people who were less likely to vote in special elections. But how?

Our entire campaign was focused on one goal—identifying approximately 11,000 "yes" votes. This figure (rounded up from 10,871) became the goal of the campaign, which was repeatedly conveyed to every volunteer through meetings, newsletters and other campaign activities. The volunteers focused on this goal, and each day we measured our progress, marking the number of identified supporters on a giant "thermometer" in the campaign office. To find 11,000 "yes" voters, we needed to find supporters among people who were likely to vote *and* people who seldom, if ever voted. We then needed to make sure each supporter voted.

The results of this careful analysis paid off. We knew the number of votes we needed to win, and on Election Day, we received 10,969 (68%) "yes" votes—almost exactly the number we predicted we needed. And we needed every one of them—this election drew a record high voter turnout of 16,130, much higher than we had initially expected.

Our victory shocked both our opposition and the press. We won because we had a good idea of who would vote and how many votes we needed to win, and we successfully ran a campaign that had a goal of getting that many votes.

On another occasion, after a successful campaign for mayor in which our client upset the incumbent mayor, the political reporter of the local newspaper wrote that our candidate was successful because voters had grown tired of the incumbent mayor. Her analysis, though creative, was totally inaccurate. Prior to the election our research had discovered that voters were very satisfied with the incumbent. We won an upset victory because we accurately estimated the number of people that were likely to vote in the election and because we were successful in "turning out to vote" additional voters who supported our candidate but were not likely to vote. Our campaign strategy had evolved *after, and only after* we figured out *how many votes* we needed to win.

To estimate the number of people likely to vote in this election, we looked at turnout from previous elections. Our polling indicated that our opponent (who was well-liked) would get at least 55% of the vote from people who were likely to vote. (She had easily won two previous elections). Our polling also indicated that *our* candidate was popular among people who were less likely to vote. If we were to have a chance of winning, we had two options: We either had to persuade voters who liked the incumbent mayor to vote against her, which would be difficult to do, *or* we needed to find other voters who had not voted previously and get them to vote for our candidate.

Given the expected low voter turnout, we felt it would be more effective to increase turnout among less likely voters than to persuade people who had previously voted for the incumbent mayor to vote for our candidate. By our calculations, we determined that if we could identify and persuade an additional 5,000 people to vote, we would win, no matter how popular the incumbent mayor was.

To win, we had to figure out how we could increase turnout among less likely voters. So we had to answer these questions:

- Why do less likely voters support our candidate? What issues are important to them?
- How difficult will it be to get these people to vote? How much volunteer effort will it take to get them out to vote? Do we have enough volunteers?
- Will our opponent attempt to increase turnout? (Meaning our estimates of the number of votes we needed could be too low.)
- How much money will need to be spent on likely voters versus unlikely voters? Do we have the ability to raise that amount of money? If so, from whom?
- Are there any voters who will support our candidate without our needing to spend significant resources on them?
- What will our opponent be likely to do to get us off of our game plan?

The answers to these questions provided us with a road map for a successful election. It all started with the analysis of how many votes we needed to win. By determining that number, our campaign strategy emerged. Our election victory was a result of implementing the strategy that began with an analysis of how many votes we needed to win.

Educators seeking to pass tax measures for their districts are surprised to learn that parents make up a surprisingly small percentage of voters, even in school tax elections. Only about one-third of parents are usually registered to vote, and of those who are registered, only about 30% of them actually vote! At best, parents may make up about 15% of the electorate in an election. Campaigning to them and ignoring the more likely voters in a community can be disastrous. Non-parents make up 85% of the voters who are registered, and older voters may represent 50-60% of likely voters in any election, yet school districts that rely on public support often make little effort to communicate with them.

The following story illustrates what can happen when you do not know who your voters are:

A large suburban school district had suffered a catastrophic defeat at the polls. The district had placed a measure on the ballot to increase funding for the schools, and voters had overwhelmingly rejected the proposal by a 3-to-1 margin. The superintendent, who had masterminded the failed effort, was at a loss to explain the defeat.

The associate superintendent (who I had previously worked with in a different school district) called me in to see if I could sort out what had happened. We met in a small, cramped district office to discuss the failed effort. Before I could ask a question, the superintendent, disappointed from the staggering loss, said he thought voters in the area were selfish and that if they wanted bad schools, then they were going to get them. I asked him what had been done to persuade voters of the need. I sat in stunned silence as he told me that his plan to pass the tax measure had been to eliminate all funds for ongoing maintenance of school buildings. He had instructed the maintenance department of the school district to ignore watering or cutting the school grass. Schools that needed painting were not painted.

"I had our maintenance department fix only those things that needed emergency attention," he said. He went on to explain his "brilliant" plan. "Because," he reasoned, "I wanted parents to see our needs every day when they brought their children to school."

He was convinced that the loss was due solely to what he described as the "stupidity of the voters."

"But that's crazy," I blurted out. I tried to explain to him that it was not parents who dominated elections but older voters. "And more often than not, despite their fixed incomes, these older voters keep their lawns neat and their homes repaired. I'll bet they were appalled that you let the schools fall into disrepair."

The superintendent was convinced he was right and could not be persuaded otherwise.

Some months later, the superintendent was fired, and a new superintendent took charge. I was again asked back to the school district to see if it would be possible to improve the district's reputation and eventually pass a bond measure to provide funds to repair the schools. It was not going to be easy, and it would take quite an effort and a long time, but the new superintendent and associate superintendent agreed to make it a priority to reach out to the voters and to listen to what they had to say.

Our first step was to analyze who voted in local elections. Not surprisingly, the largest group were older voters. Parents made up a small percentage of likely voters—barely 18%. Through a series of community meetings and questionnaires that we mailed to voters (not just parents), we asked people why they had voted no. What they told us was that the previous superintendent's strategy had backfired, and voters were angry at the school district.

"Can't you even cut the grass?" one man complained.

The older voters who had come out in droves to vote against the tax measure told us they could not trust the district with more money, if the district could not even keep the schools repaired. We were told that the poorly maintained schools reflected poorly on their neighborhoods, and voters were not about to vote for more money for more of the same. The superintendent's "brilliant idea" had completely misfired.

It was clear that it was going to take a lot of time and a lot of effort to repair the damage that had been done.

The associate superintendent, with the support of the Board of Education and the new superintendent, developed a plan to fix each school as best they could with limited funds and recruited volunteers from the community to help. On weekends and afternoons, volunteers pitched in to water the lawns and cut the grass. Other volunteers helped paint classrooms. Meanwhile, as the repairs were being completed, the superintendent and business manager continued to communicate with older voters as well as with parents through letters and newsletters, phone calls and occasional community meetings. The district applied for all available funds, and they did as much as they could on their own.

For five full years, we worked with the district to improve the schools and to increase public support. Gradually, almost imperceptibly, support grew, along with an understanding of the real needs of the district. While the district was eager to put a measure on the ballot, as the money was critically needed, we had to have patience and allow the public support and trust of the school district to be rebuilt.

Five years after the failed measure, a new measure was placed on the ballot. Many of our campaign volunteers were the same seniors who had been opposed to the previous measure. This time, the bond measure gained support from all sides—even the local taxpayer watchdog group endorsed it, and on Election Day, the measure won with a 70% "yes" vote.

By identifying the likely voters in their community, and by communicating with them and listening to their concerns, the district was able to build support where there had been distrust. Voters, although few of them had school-aged children, voted to increase their taxes to support the school district. Even after that election, the district continued to communicate with ALL voters, not just parents. They communicated to them when there was good news to share and when the news was not so good. They kept the public informed of progress in the renovation of the schools and the schedule for completion of the projects. Today, relations with the community have never been better. It started with an understanding of who votes.

Sometimes, when figuring out how many votes you need to win, you realize that there are not enough potential supporters for you to win. In that case, you have to find more voters. How? Register them and then get them out to vote.

A city council candidate we worked with finished second in a four-person race for city council. Our opponent, who had finished first, narrowly missed receiving the necessary votes to win outright. Since city rules required the winner to receive 50%+1 of the vote, we faced an uphill battle in a run-off election.

To win, we needed to do more than just run a better campaign. We determined we needed to get additional voters to the polls. Over the summer months, our candidate and volunteers went door-to-door in the district explaining to citizens, who were not registered to vote, that the city government would be more responsive to their neighborhood needs if they voted. We explained that political power begins with voting, and that if they wanted better street lighting and improved police protection, they needed to vote. At every opportunity, we registered anyone who was not registered to vote.

By the end of the summer, we had registered over 1000 new voters—many were immigrants and new American citizens and had never voted before. When Election Day came, we made a decision to devote time and effort reminding people to vote and explaining the voting process to these new voters. While not all of them made it to the polls, enough did that we were able to win the election, shocking our opponent and his supporters.

Chapter Nine

Develop a Plan

No prudent traveler would seriously consider taking a road trip across the United States without a road map and an idea of where to stop, where to eat and how much money it will take to reach the destination. There are countless decisions to be made before taking off to ensure the trip is safe and successful.

A political campaign also needs a plan, a road map if you will, before beginning. Some campaign plans are written on the backs of napkins, others are complex and have detailed analyses of voters, the competition, and potential messages. Timelines, budgets, polling information and communication strategies may all be part of a sophisticated campaign plan.

For years I kept campaign plans in my head and did not provide them in written form to my clients. But over the years, I have learned that the more people that are aware of the campaign plan and have bought into the overall concept of the plan, the better. I would never think of traveling across the country with my family without discussing the particulars of the trip with them and making proper preparations. Likewise, the campaign plan needs to be reviewed by all those who will have a role in the implementation of it. By doing so, you avoid misunderstandings that can result in everyone wanting to go in a different direction.

Campaign plans and objectives generally should evolve from an estimate of the number of votes that it will take to win the election and then the number of votes each candidate is likely to receive. This can be done through polling or from a careful analysis of previous elections. Once estimates are done, the strategies emerge on how to achieve vote targets. The easiest way to lose an election is to not know how many votes you need to win and to not have a plan to achieve those votes.

There are three critical factors to consider in developing a campaign plan:

1) Understand what type of election you are in.

Think of it like any game where you must understand the rules, and the first rule is to learn the rules of your election. Ask yourself a series of questions:

- Is it a regular or special election? A statewide or local election? Is it an "off year" election or a general election?
- Based on the election type, what specific percent of the vote is required to win?
- Will there be a runoff?
- Are there multiple candidates?
- Are there other issues on the ballot, or is your measure/election the only thing on the ballot?
- Is absentee voting allowed?
- Will voting take place on one day or on multiple days?
- What day will the election be held? (Some states vote on Saturdays others on Tuesdays).

Who votes in a particular election is largely determined by the type of election. That is because voting, like making your bed, is a habit. Some people do it religiously, some rarely, and others never do it. Depending on the type of election, you can estimate how many people will vote. Just look at the turnout from previous elections of that type in your area as a guide for what it is likely to be in the future.

Here are some general guidelines on the level of turnout in different elections:

- Presidential elections have the highest turnout, special elections usually the lowest.
- The turnout will usually be higher in statewide elections than in local elections, since many people who turn out for statewide elections do not vote in local elections.
- The turnout will usually be higher for a regularly scheduled election, particularly when there are a variety of candidates and issues to vote

for, rather than a special election, with only one or a few candidates or issues.

- The turnout will be higher if there is a matter of controversy to be decided, particularly if it has received significant press coverage; the turnout will be much lower if it is a routine election and there is not much public discussion or controversy.

2) Calculate the number of votes you need to win.

It is not difficult to determine how many people are likely to vote in any election if you take the time to do a little research. The effort expended at the beginning of the campaign to estimate this number and to determine what percent of the turnout of voters you need will provide the campaign with a road map to measure progress along the way.

Are there multiple candidates? How many votes do you anticipate other candidates receiving? How will this information affect your plans? Does your election require a super majority or a simple majority to win? Try to calculate the specific number of votes you need rather than a percentage. It is more meaningful to know that you need 15,000 votes to win rather than 50%+1.

3) Figure out how you are going to get the votes you need.

Of the likely voters, how many of them are likely to vote for you? Do you need to register new voters? Will you need to motivate people to vote who are less likely to vote? How much money will be needed? How will money be spent communicating to voters? When will the money be spent? The effective utilization of resources—money, people and time—are the keys to getting the votes you need to win, and your campaign plan should address each one of these important resources:

Money. Local campaigns rarely have unlimited resources. Determining how much money can be raised and when it can be raised needs to be addressed in the campaign plan. The campaign will need to make choices on how and on what the money will be spent. Like a family that has limited income, difficult decisions will need to be made as to priorities for spending. Everyone will have their own ideas of how money should be spent and making good financial decisions is essential.

Remember: The only people who matter are those who take the time to vote, therefore campaign dollars must be spent on those activities that reach voters.

People. A campaign plan should delineate the various responsibilities of the people involved in the campaign. If there is paid staff, how many will be needed? What are their responsibilities? The responsibilities of the consultant (if there is one), the finance director, the candidate and the campaign committee need to be written. If volunteers are needed, there needs to be an understanding as to what they will be doing and when. How will their efforts contribute to the victory?

Time. Political campaigns have a finite amount of time. The clock starts when you begin and ends when the polls close on Election Day. It may be 365 days or 65 days or 90 days or 123 days or 37 days or 10 days. It is important to know exactly how many days you have and develop a plan to use *every day* to make progress. The campaign plan should be detailed enough to provide monthly objectives to measure progress toward the goal. "Managing the clock," determining how much time you have, understanding what you need to do and when to communicate to voters are all essential parts of winning.

* * * * *

No campaign I have been involved in over the years, be it a political campaign or an organizing campaign or a PR campaign, went exactly as originally planned. Each had its ups and downs. I have learned that it is important to acknowledge at the beginning of the campaign that there will be some unexpected setbacks along the way. Modifications and adjustments of the initial plan will need to be made as the campaign unfolds and as the opposition implements their strategy or the public reacts to what is being done. By anticipating setbacks, it is possible to keep some perspective and to guard against overreacting when things do not go as planned.

Once a campaign is moving, it is sometimes necessary to change plans midstream. Campaign plans are made weeks, even months, before Election Day. What seemed like a good idea during the summer before the attack ads from the opposition hit, might not seem so good now. Campaign strategies and plans have to be continually adapted as the campaign unfolds. It is not unlike the work of a military strategist who has to adjust plans once the war begins. You must be ready to drop everything in order to take advantage of opportunities or challenges as they come.

The similarities between political campaigns and military campaigns are numerous. Both require detailed planning. Both take significant resources. Both take a financial commitment. Both take a physical and mental toll on the participants. In both, the risks are high and the potential for loss great. Both are likely to suffer some defeats and problems along the way to victory. Success usually comes to the best prepared, the strongest, the most committed, the most nimble and the most able to turn adversity into an advantage. Both require strong leadership. Both require strict organizational discipline.

While there are similarities between political campaigns and military campaigns, the biggest difference is the "use of the clock." A military campaign may take days, weeks, months or even years, but a political campaign is won or lost on one day—Election Day—and timing is everything.

Chapter Ten

Timing is Everything

Timing is everything in politics. The Olympic games are held every four years. In the four years between the Games, athletes train with one objective: getting mentally and physically prepared to perform at their peak for that critical moment or event. The difference between gold and silver or winning and losing is usually the smallest of margins. Athletes train themselves to peak at the proper time, not too soon or too late.

In politics, peaking at the proper time is an art form and is the result of careful strategy and planning. People involved in losing campaigns often say, "If I had one more week, I would have won." or "Had the election been held last week, we would have won."

What they are saying is their campaigns did not peak at the proper time.

Sometimes events cannot be controlled. In San Francisco, a campaign to build a ballpark was lost because an earthquake struck a couple of weeks before the election, and voters' priorities shifted. In Los Angeles, a major candidate for city council was unsuccessful because he was dependent on an effective "Get out the Vote" (GOTV) among senior citizens. Unfortunately, few seniors wanted to vote that day. The date of the election: September 11, 2001.

These are the exceptions. Usually, it is possible to use time to your advantage. It is not the hare who wins the race, rather the tortoise that keeps going step-after-step. Knowing how much time is available is the first step in developing a winning campaign. Using time, pacing yourself as well as the tempo of the campaign becomes a critical necessity in managing a successful campaign.

In the UFW, we were faced with a struggle that we knew would take years to be successful. There was no time frame. We did not know if we would be successful in 2 years, 5 years or longer. To keep people motivated, it was necessary to create goals for our supporters and for ourselves. At one point, my local staff made a goal to distribute 50,000 leaflets about the grape boycott at local shopping centers. We then set a new goal of distributing 100,000 leaflets after we reached the previous goal (which took several weeks of intense work). When that goal was reached, we upped it to 250,000, then a million. By the time we had distributed 1,000,000 leaflets, we were pretty well-convinced that most of the people in the community had heard about the boycott. Then, we said we would collect 50,000 signatures of people who pledged not to buy grapes as part of our boycott. We went to the supermarkets once we collected the signatures and asked them to remove the grapes because 50,000 of their consumers had pledged to support our boycott. Setting and reaching arbitrary goals became a tool for motivating people and making progress.

Once you know how much time you have available, a plan must be made to determine what needs to be done and when it should be done. The sequence in which your plan unfolds will affect your ability to manage time.

I recently was hired to direct a mayoral campaign in a large city. While the campaign had been in gear for some weeks prior to my hiring, the campaign team had no plan for using the time available—hoping whatever they did would eventually lead to an election victory. Obviously, there was no momentum, and staff and volunteers had little direction or motivation. To get things on track, we first set five goals of what we wanted to accomplish in the next *two weeks,* with one of our goals being the development of month-by-month objectives.

We also made a decision, not a popular one, to eliminate voter contact for a month until we figured out how many votes we needed to win and from what areas of the city we could get those votes. Knowing who to communicate to would save time and effort in the long run. Effectively managing time requires clear priorities and a commitment to follow those priorities.

Peaking is the art of bringing all campaign efforts (mail, volunteer activity, TV, voter contact and message) together when voters are making their decision who or what to vote for. Mary Hughes, a respected political consultant, likens a political campaign to a Broadway play, describing it as ten months of practice and then it is showtime. A campaign should attempt to peak close to Election Day, and the tempo and pace of the campaign should start slowly and build to a crescendo on Election Day. A campaign that peaks too early will usually fail.

Candidates and inexperienced campaigners often think that voters are as interested in the election as they are. They are not. The majority of voters do not start paying attention to elections until the last few weeks before the election, perhaps just a few days before the election. Voters have many other things on their minds, and election issues and decisions are generally not at the top of most voters concerns.

In a desire to "educate the electorate," some campaigners scramble to get the first piece of mail out to voters months or weeks before the election, falsely thinking that getting a jump on the opposition will be of some advantage. Voters do not keep track of who joined the campaign first or who mailed first or who was on TV first. What matters is what is communicated to them at the time they are making a decision.

In a recent election, a campaign manager, faced with an early March election, sent campaign mail and then had follow-up phone calls made to voters in mid December. She was shocked when voters complained about receiving political calls right before Christmas. Had the election been in November, calls made eight to ten weeks before might have been acceptable. Calls eight to ten weeks before a March election, at Christmas time, were totally unacceptable.

I am often asked: How much time do we need to campaign? or When should we get started? There are no set rules. Lack of time usually is not the biggest problem, wasting time is. How is it wasted? By not working evenings and weekends. By not having clear goals and daily meetings to keep the campaign on track. By avoiding making critical decisions and by continually changing strategies.

Creating a sense of urgency can help build momentum. Campaigns are a series of mini crises managed in an effective way to build momentum. The effective organizer uses goals and events to get people involved.

"Kick-offs," "emergency" meetings, weekly mobilizations, strategy sessions and house meetings can all be used to draw people into the campaign and inspire them to volunteer their time. A boulder pushed down a hill creates its own momentum. The difficulty is getting the boulder moving initially. A campaign has the same problem. Urgency has to be created.

During Barbara Boxer's upset victory for the U.S. Senate, we had thousands of volunteers around the state working to get out the vote. Because polls on the East Coast close three hours before those on the West Coast, we were worried that many of our supporters would not vote, thinking their vote now did not matter. We knew that TV analysts would declare a victor in the presidential election hours before the polls closed in California and the announcement would have the affect of discouraging voters living on the West Coast to vote.

To counter this anticipated 5 P.M. TV announcement we called every campaign volunteer in the state (over 50,000 of them) using an elaborate phone tree and told them that we had learned one of the TV networks had done an exit poll, and Barbara Boxer was losing narrowly.

We urged people to work feverishly up to the last minute "pulling out" every vote possible. We urged our volunteers to tell voters that Barbara was going to lose unless they voted. It worked. Barbara won by a mere 10 votes per precinct. In many of our precincts, we had turned out to vote 20–30 people between 5 P.M. and 8 P.M. who would not have voted without the persistence of the volunteers.

Barbara's victory was due in part to our ability to increase turnout. We were able to do this because the campaign recognized months earlier the necessity of having volunteers ready and trained to do an effective get-out-the-vote, but they needed a sense of urgency for the final push for victory. Our emergency call at 5 P.M. made the difference.

* * * * *

Art Agnos's election as mayor of San Francisco was regarded at the time as a major upset. The assassination of Mayor George Moscone along with gay Supervisor Harvey Milk nine years earlier had left progressives in San Francisco (neighborhood activists, gays, labor unions and ethnic minorities) isolated from what they perceived as the centrist/downtown dominated mayoral administration of Dianne Feinstein. To many, Art Agnos represented the best chance of beating her popular heir apparent and San Francisco native son, Supervisor John Molinari.

Some nine months before the election, I found myself waiting to be interviewed by Agnos in his San Francisco office. Richard Ross, Agnos's long time political advisor and close friend, had recommended me to Agnos. Ross and I had worked together years earlier in the UFW, and after he left the

Union, Ross developed quite a reputation for managing successful political campaigns. Upon occasion, Ross "drafted" me into building "field operations" in a number of close elections after I left the UFW.

My reputation at the time was that of a tough disciplined union organizer. Having spent 11 years in the UFW working with Cesar Chavez, I was accustomed to demanding leaders and difficult campaigns. As I sat in Art's office, I noticed the deferential way his staff treated him. It was clear he liked things HIS way, from his impeccable groomed suits to his Grecian formula tinted hair with a trace of distinguished gray and the precisely placed miniature replicas of the Statue of Liberty on his desk. This was no democracy I was being interviewed to be a part of, it was a campaign that he intended to win on his way to bigger and better things. He was not concerned with his recent dismal poll numbers, his lack of San Francisco pedigree, the popularity of incumbent Mayor Feinstein or her popular hand-picked choice to succeed her. Above all, Art believed in himself. He intended to win this election, and he was assembling a team of people to help him.

We talked for about an hour—mostly about him. His immigrant parents, his move to San Francisco years earlier as a young social worker and his love of baseball. We talked about empowering people who are often left out of the political process. He was interested in how organizing worked and how it could be used to build support for causes that needed popular and political support. Mostly, we talked about how grassroots organizing could help him win the mayor's race.

He asked me what I would need to work for him. I think he wanted to know what I wanted to be paid. I ignored that question and told him I would need his support on three things. First, I needed time and support to build an army of volunteers. We had to get started immediately. Second, I needed to recruit a talented staff that would commit themselves to working harder and longer than they had ever worked before. Finally, I needed his personal commitment that *no matter what* he would support these things, and he had to commit to attending volunteer meetings every Saturday, without fail.

I explained that these Saturday meetings would be the cornerstone of our grass roots campaign. It would be a time where volunteers, not the rich, financial contributors or special interests, could meet with Art, ask him questions, meet other volunteers, report successes and failures. We would come together each week to measure our progress, to be accountable to each

Framed by "stars"– names of people who volunteered–Senator
Alan Cranston, Larry Tramutola and Art Agnos discuss Art's
campaign for Mayor.

other and to build the campaign from the ground up.

Art agreed to my modest demands, we shook hands, and I left not knowing the important lessons I would later learn in this campaign.

We began our efforts calling people from any list of supporters we could find: people whom Art had helped over the years as a social worker, family members, nurses who worked with Art's sister in the California Nurses Association, senior activists, Chinese, Latino and Filipino clubs, artists, union members and tenants.

At first it was slow. Not accustomed to disciplined work, many people came one week and not the next, but slowly, over time, the numbers of volunteers grew.

Our Saturday meetings became like religious events. We reported what we had accomplished the previous week and what our plans were for the next. We had reports of what our opposition was doing, we sang and applauded when someone was introduced. Food was donated by one group or another. Our schedule was always the same. Start the meeting at 10 A.M. sharp, an hour of talk, music, reports and then dispatch out to the neighborhoods to leaflet, walk precincts and talk to voters. We returned at 3 or 4 in the afternoon, tired, sun burned or cold to a warm meal and a "wrap up" meeting where people reported on what they had accomplished and what questions voters had. Volunteers were thanked and asked to come again the following week.

We developed friendships. We learned who were the real workers and who were the talkers. All volunteers had their names printed on a colorful star hanging from the ceiling, so looking up each week we could see more stars and more people who had joined the campaign. Some weeks were more difficult than others. Occasionally, only a few people showed up. Maybe it was too cold and rainy, or maybe we had not done a good enough job as organizers, but we never canceled a Saturday meeting. Whoever came was dispatched out to talk to voters.

There were times we did not want to meet, like when Jelani Everhart, the nine-year-old son of Art's chief of staff, was tragically killed by a truck while riding on his bicycle in front of his house or when an elderly campaign volunteer died. Yet every Saturday, without fail, we met, we talked, we laughed, we cried and we kept at it.

In May, our campaign was rocked by a report in the San Francisco Chronicle that Art failed to pay income tax on $65,000 profit from a land speculation deal arranged by a Sacramento developer named in a political corruption case. Then, in July, we got news of a new story that was to be published detailing new errors Agnos had made in his tax statement. Art was devastated. Richard Ross, his closest friend and savvy advisor, said the campaign was over, we could not recover. The report was to hit the Saturday papers. On Friday night, at about 11 P.M., I got a frantic call at home from CJ Maupin, one of our senior campaign workers. She said Art was in the headquarters, but he was heading to Sacramento. He did not want to talk to the press and was planning to drop out of the race and Ross, who was in Las Vegas, could not be reached. I told CJ to keep Art in the office until I could get over to the headquarters and talk to him.

When I arrived, the headquarters was abandoned except for CJ, Art and a couple of organizers who were finishing up work. Art was slouched on a couch in a 2nd floor office that looked down upon the multi-colored stars and the meeting room where we had our Saturday mobilizations. "It's over." Art said. "There is no way we can recover from this. It's bullshit, the Chronicle is going out of its way to help Molinari."

We talked for a while. Mostly, I listened. When he was done I said: "Months ago, when you interviewed me, I said I needed three things. One of those things you promised me was that you would show up *every* Saturday, without fail. You promised me, and I am holding you to that promise. Look out at the stars, Art. Every one represents a person who has volunteered their precious time. It's not about you anymore, it's about them. You owe it to them to come, to answer their questions. To keep going. We have four months to recover. Time is on our side."

Saturday morning came. On the front page of the Chronicle was a searing article about Art and his tax troubles. At 10 A.M., our volunteers showed up, as always, not knowing what to expect. About 5 minutes after 10, Art came in wearing his blue and red Rugby shirt. "Let's talk," he said. "I think you need to know what the Chronicle didn't write." For an hour, Art answered the tough questions. He took responsibility, said he made a mistake and would make others. He would learn from his mistakes and be better for it.

We dispatched those who would go out to hand out Agnos brochures to voters. I remember going to Potrero Hill, one of our strongholds because I wanted to hear what our "supporters" would say. It was brutal that Saturday. Many said, "He's a crook" or "He's a bum." Some listened, some said, "I'll think about it."

We came back to the headquarters. We talked about what people had said and what we had learned. We kept on. The campaign had taken a hard hit, but we were still standing. Over the next several months, more people joined our campaign. More stars were hung from the ceiling.

We eventually won the mayor's race, building the largest grass roots army in the history of San Francisco. Over 2,500 volunteers walked precincts, phoned voters and hand delivered, in seven days, 100,000 copies of Art's book "Getting Things Done."

The San Francisco Examiner described the Agnos victory as "stunning." On election night and the day after, one by one, volunteers came to the office and claimed their stars. We had learned a lot. We learned that our success was due to the efforts of hundreds of people. Volunteers kept the faith and sustained us. The victory could not have happened without them. We learned about time and using it to our advantage. We kept at it. We never quit. We learned some great lessons:

Keep working every day. Slow and steady wins the race.

Campaigns are more like a marathon rather than a sprint. Effort needs to be made to peak at the right time and to pace the campaign for a long sustained effort. Starting fast and ending slow is not a formula for success. A campaign needs to be structured so that all actions peak at the right time. In business, it is possible to be successful without the necessity of "peaking," doing a good job day after day is sufficient. In political campaigns, it is essential that all activities peak at the same time that people are making their decision on how they will vote.

Tomorrow is a new day, a new beginning. Success usually goes to those that keep at it day after day and to those who have the commitment to keep going despite difficulties. Investment advisors will advise investors not to panic when the market drops. The same advice is valuable for candidates and for those running issue campaigns. Do not panic when the market is down. Do not panic when the campaign is not going well. Success comes to those who keep at it.

Obstacles and setbacks are normal and to be expected. Most campaigns suffer setbacks at some stage along the way. During the campaign itself, it is

Mayor elect, Art Agnos, discussing his upset victory with me and Press Secretary, Scott Shafer, on Election Night. The San Francisco Examiner described Agnos's victory as "stunning." We built the largest grassroots army in the history of San Francisco. Over 2,500 volunteers walked precincts, phoned voters and in seven days, hand delivered 100,000 copies of Art's book *Getting Things Done.*

difficult to have any perspective as to what might be fatal. A negative press article might have less effect than you think. A gaff of one type or another may be important only to a few. Rarely is an election loss due to one specific event or action. Obstacles and setbacks are healthy as long as they are not over-analyzed and over-reacted to.

Once you make a commitment to run, keep at it, even when things are not going well. Campaigns involve many different people who get involved for many different reasons. Some are volunteering for the first time, others have been motivated by particular issues. Once a candidate makes a commitment to run, she owes it to the volunteers and others who are also sacrificing for the cause to keep going all the way to the end, win or lose.

Never quit. There is more shame in quitting than in losing. In marathon races, the last place finisher is still applauded. The person who quits is forgotten. Campaigns are about raising issues, involving people in the political process and forcing the opposition to deal with issues they may not want to deal with. Quitting short-circuits the process and everyone loses.

Do not celebrate before election results are in. Campaigns can be lost in the final days or the final hours on Election Day. The surest way to lose is to think you have won before the votes are counted. Every minute counts and every vote matters.

Chapter Eleven

One Vote Can Make a Difference

One single vote can be the difference between winning and losing an election. Local elections are *often* decided by just a few votes. Our firm has helped almost 200 public agencies pass bonds and new taxes, and we have helped over 200 people win races to elected office. Many of these "wins" were won by just a percent or two. Regrettably, we have also lost a few elections—but in these, just a few votes usually marked the difference between winning and losing.

That is what happened when I ran a campaign in the San Ramon Valley School District, an affluent suburb about 20 miles east of San Francisco. The goal was to pass a tax measure to provide funds to repair and renovate the district's aging schools, and we needed 66.7% of the vote to win. We campaigned hard, and over 30,000 people voted on the measure; however, when the votes were counted, we received 66.6% of the vote, not the 66.7% then required by California law. We lost by just 2 *votes*.

In our post election analysis, we discovered that many parents, grandparents, teachers, and school administrators—all of whom had *told* us they were going to vote "yes"—had not found the time to vote. Others, who voted by mail, sent their ballots in late, and their votes were not counted. Because some people did not take the time or thought their vote did not matter, the measure lost at the ballot, and the community lost the opportunity to renovate their district's aging schools.

One parent said, "I intended to vote, but I just lost track of time."

A teacher told us, "I never thought my one vote was needed. We hear all the time that voting doesn't matter. Now I know it does."

A grandparent lamented, "I'm so embarrassed. I just can't believe I didn't find time to vote."

This story fortunately has a happy ending. Rather than be discouraged, school leaders ran a new campaign and made sure every supporter voted. They had learned their lesson, and they won with a 77% "yes" vote.

* * * * *

Voter turnout continues to decline nationwide, and today, at best, only 3 out of 10 people who are registered to vote actually vote in local or municipal elections. Registered voters only make up a small percent of those eligible to vote. Young people particularly are becoming more difficult to convince of the importance of voting.

I saw an example of this when I was helping collect signatures to qualify an initiative for the ballot that, if successful, would provide funds to expand the City of Oakland's zoo, renovate the Oakland Museum and provide for an expansion of the popular public Chabot Space and Science Center.

While collecting signatures on a busy street corner in the middle class Piedmont Avenue area of Oakland, I approached a young couple pushing their young child in a stroller. "Are you registered to vote?" I asked. "Would you like to sign this petition? It's to put a measure on the ballot to provide additional funds to renovate our local zoo, museum and science center."

"We're not registered to vote, and we're not interested in voting," the young man said firmly.

"Why not?" I asked.

"Because we're disgusted by both parties," he said, as his wife beside him nodded her head in agreement. "Politicians say one thing and then do what they want. Besides, our two votes won't make a difference," he concluded.

"This is not about the political parties, it's about *our* community," I said. "Your two votes could make a huge difference not only in this election but other elections. You may not be interested in the zoo or the museum, but your child will be going to school soon. Who you elect to the local Board of Education will affect him."

They paused, and for a second I thought I had persuaded them. But instead they said, "No we're not interested."

I tried to convince them but they walked on, choosing to be indifferent and unaware of the importance politics and voting has on their lives.

As the day wore on, I found their response was not uncommon. Many people were not registered to vote and did not want to register. Others who were registered did not want to sign the petition. The usual reason for not registering to vote or signing our petition was that they "didn't want to be bothered." Although I collected many signatures that day, I knew that statistically (with less than 3 out of 10 registered voters actually voting) many of the people who actually had signed my petition probably would not make it to the polls.

Yet, with voter turnout at its lowest level in years, especially in local elections, *one single* vote can be critically important in determining who sits on the school board, whether tax measures to fix and repair schools get passed or whether hospitals remain open. And despite discouraging trends in voter participation, there are countless examples where a few votes have made a positive difference.

A few miles from the street corner where the young couple decided not to register to vote, a hospital was saved from closure by just a handful of votes and the tireless work of volunteers, mostly senior citizens. As part of their campaign to save their local hospital, senior citizen volunteers called every likely voter, explaining the importance of keeping the emergency room open and the hardship it would cause if the hospital closed. As Election Day neared, it was clear the vote would be close (66.7% was needed for passage). Everything depended on getting identified supporters out to vote.

On the day of the election, volunteers put all their efforts into getting people to the polls. From early in the morning until the polls closed at 8 P.M., they did everything they could—they drove people to the polls, made phone calls to encourage the sick and elderly to get out of bed to go vote, they went door-to-door to encourage people to vote. They told each potential voter how much their individual vote mattered. At 8 P.M., the polls closed, and there was no more anyone could do except wait for the outcome. Finally, the results came in, and by the narrowest of margins—less than 6 votes per precinct—they won. The volunteers were tired and exhausted but overjoyed. Their hospital was saved from closure, and each of them knew that they had directly helped save it. Their efforts had made a difference. They needed every vote they got to win, and every volunteer had contributed to the victory.

Curtis Gans, director of the Committee for the Study of the American Electorate and an expert on voting participation in the United States, reports that voter turnout today is 50% lower than it was in the 1960s and 1970s. In March 2002, turnout achieved by both political parties combined was a mere 16% of the eligible voters.

According to Gans, decline in voting is occurring in every race, gender and income group in the United States. Inasmuch as voting is the one tangible way the public can make their voice heard by elected officials, the fact that most people do not vote means fewer and fewer people influence policies and decisions that affect the lives of many.

Whether turned off by politicians, too busy to vote, too lazy to participate or too self-absorbed, Americans could learn a lot from other countries whose right to vote is not taken for granted.

* * * * *

In 1993, I traveled to South Africa to provide assistance and training to South Africans who were preparing to vote for the first time. By November 1993, change was happening in South Africa. Nelson Mandela had been released from prison, and as a result of worldwide pressure, the South African government had reluctantly agreed to schedule elections to be held at a not-yet-determined date the following year. I had been selected to participate in a conference in Johannesburg sponsored by the Joint Center for Political and Economic Studies. I was one of several Americans who would speak about electoral organizing. I was not worried about encouraging people to vote. The election would mark the official end of apartheid, and the anticipation and excitement of the upcoming election was on the minds of everyone.

As I waited to speak, I looked out upon the faces of the delegates in the packed conference room of the Protea Hotel. The room was made up of representatives from the various (previously banned) political parties. None of them, I realized, had *ever* voted, not because they had not wanted to or because they did not have the time, but because under South African, law they had been *forbidden* to vote.

When my turn came to address the delegates, rather than give my prepared speech about electoral organizing, I decided to pose them a number of questions—questions they energetically struggled to answer:

- "How old do you have to be to vote?" The answers to this and many other questions had not yet been decided.
- "How many polling places do you need?" Just one polling place had

been proposed for Alexandria. I mentioned that in San Francisco we have over 800 polling places to handle roughly the same population. It was clear that one polling place could not accommodate the number of people who would be voting, and plans needed to be made to make sure the government added additional polling places.

- "When will polls open in the morning? When will they close in the evening?"
- "Over how many days will the election be held?"
- "Have you thought of how to keep people in lines if there is a long wait?
- "What do you plan to do if there is intimidation?"
- "How will people know who to vote for? Many can't read."

Our discussion was lively, and when I told them that many Americans rarely vote and many say their votes don't matter, the delegates were incredulous.

At the end of one of the sessions, one of the delegates came up to us and asked us if we would like to see his community where he had been organizing. "And would you speak to the people there about how you have organized voters in America?" he asked.

The next day we went to his home in Alexandria, a squalid township on the outskirts of Johannesburg. Like many black townships, built on the fringes of modern cities to house the thousands of black South African laborers, Alexandria was a community of huts and shanties with no running water, little or no electricity and open trenches for sewage, which spilled into the dry creek and washes. Each day, the workers would get up before sunrise and walk from their corrugated tin huts and shanties to work in the homes of wealthy white South Africans and in the white owned businesses and factories. In the evening, they would return to the shanties and squalor of Alexandria.

Despite these desperate conditions, people had hope that the upcoming election would be a step towards building a new South Africa based on principles of democracy and equality. Already, schools were emerging, housing co-ops were starting and plans were being made to bring electricity and water to people for the first time. Hope was flourishing throughout the country. On a taxicab window, I saw that someone had etched Martin Luther King Jr.'s picture and the words of his "I have a dream" speech. We saw houses barely large enough to fit a table and a bed with pictures of Nelson Mandela and Martin Luther King Jr. pinned on the walls.

At lunchtime, we stopped at a makeshift community center. There were hundreds of old people, men and women, sitting together eating lunch under tarps and tents to protect them from the hot December sun. "Today is Senior Citizen Day," our guide told us, explaining the large gathering. "Each Wednesday, senior citizens come to hear the news of what is happening in our country. Today, we are going to talk about the elections. They have never voted before, and they want to learn how."

Awed and humbled by the scene, we were each introduced as Americans who had come to support democracy in South Africa and to advise them on elections. As our guide translated our words, each of us spoke briefly about how proud we were to be with them as they approached their historic elections. When we were done, the crowd stood as one and sang "Mother Africa" in their native tongue.

When we were leaving, a white-haired, old man, his back stooped and his faced wrinkled by years of hard work, came up to us and told us, "I'm 102 years old now, and I've spent 20 years in prison because of my opposition to apartheid. I'm not sure how much longer I'm going to live, probably not long, but I'm going to make sure I live long enough to vote at least once. Then, once I have voted, I can die knowing I cast my vote in a *free* South Africa."

I have remembered that man many times as I speak to people encouraging them to vote. The right to vote is the cornerstone of democracy and freedom. Thousands of men and women have died throughout our history fighting to protect the democracy and freedom we so easily take for granted.

I wish that the couple I met on Piedmont Avenue who refused to register to vote could have seen that event or heard the voice of the man who spent 20 years in prison and lived long enough to cast his ballot.

Voting is a responsibility we all have if we are to live in a free society. As my South African friend in Alexandria told me, **"The greatest thing you Americans export is not your technology, your grain or your consumer products. Your greatest export to the world is Democracy, and you don't even know it."**

* * * * *

Every U.S. citizen becomes eligible to vote at eighteen years old. Fewer than 20% of us who are over 18 actually exercise that right. Many of us take for granted the right to vote, yet over 2 *billion* people in the world do not

This 102-year-old South African voted for the first time in the historic South African elections in 1994. He told the gathering, "I'm not sure how long I'm going to live ... but I'm going to make sure I live long enough to vote. Then, once I have voted, I can die knowing I cast my vote for a *free* South Africa."

even have that right! Voting for our elected representatives is a precious right in our country, yet fewer and fewer of us participate in the electoral process. We hear complaints that schools are not good, roads are not repaired and elected officials care only about "special interests," yet many of the people who complain the loudest do not make the effort to vote.

Getting people to vote is sometimes difficult. People often need to be reminded to vote on Election Day. Despite their best intentions, many people forget to vote, get too busy or think their vote does not matter.

Fred Ross used to say: "Reminding is the essence of organizing." Voter turnout can increase 5% or more with a targeted and effective effort to remind people to vote. These extra votes can often be the difference between winning and losing. Today, most campaigns do not devote much effort into getting people to vote. It's a mistake. Get-Out-The-Vote (GOTV) efforts, if properly funded and organized, can provide the critical margin needed to win.

Historically, getting people to exercise their right to vote was a primary concern of political parties. For over 150 years, political parties were engaged in extensive efforts to ensure that voters loyal to the party voted. For example, in St. Louis at the turn of the century, volunteers were positioned at each polling place to check the names of people who came in to vote. This person was called a "scratcher," and he would be responsible for scratching off the names of the registered voters who came to vote. As the day went on and some people did not vote, another volunteer was dispatched to the home of the person who had not yet voted to persuade them to come to vote.

In South Africa, their first presidential elections were conducted over a two-day period, to ensure the maximum participation. In most of the United States, Election Day is one day, usually a Tuesday—a workday for most. In some states, Election Day is Saturday. Some states have gone to "mail only" elections. Absentee voting and other reforms to allow citizens to vote early at designated sites have helped make it easier to vote, but most voters still vote on Election Day, and the majority of them vote between 4 P.M. and the close of polls (usually 8P.M.).

Little effort is made by the political parties to involve less likely voters in the political process. They receive no mail, no phone calls, and no one is likely to ask their opinion since opinion polls also target likely voters. In short, less frequent voters are normally ignored by campaigns and become irrelevant. If young voters, minority voters and low income voters make up most of the unlikely voters, their opinions and perspectives also become irrelevant.

The Republican Party, at the national level, is winning more close races because of their investment in GOTV efforts. Long an effective strategy of the Democratic Party, the Republicans, under the leadership of the former Christian Coalition Director Ralph Reed, have revitalized their grass roots outreach. As the New York Times reported, "In Georgia ... Minnesota, Colorado, South Dakota and more than 25 other states ... Republicans have recruited more volunteers, made more telephone calls, rang more doorbells and got out more votes in Republican households than they ever had."

The success the Republicans are having in what was once a Democratic strength came after a Republican National Committee study showed that Democrats out-performed at the polls by increasing turnout in Get-Out-The-Vote campaigns in key races. The Republicans spent significant sums of money and effort improving their grassroots capability, and the effort is paying off.

A campaign that does not develop a GOTV strategy generally loses if the vote is close. An effective GOTV effort has these FOUR common elements:

You must know who to get out to vote. Obviously, you only want to encourage people to vote who are likely to support your candidate or your cause. Identifying supporters throughout the campaign allows you to focus GOTV efforts on those who support you.

You must have sufficient Election Day volunteers. You need enough volunteers who are able to call and visit every voter (multiple times) to encourage them to vote. Encouraging people to vote is hard work. Personal attention is essential to motivate people to vote.

Election Day GOTV volunteers must be persistent. It takes constant reminding to get people to vote. One reminder usually does not do it. Unfortunately, the people less likely to vote need to be pushed, prodded and pulled.

Election Day volunteers must work all the way up to the time polls close. In a close election, the people who are encouraged to vote at the last minute could very well decide the election.

While every vote matters and countless elections are decided by a handful of votes, it is nevertheless becoming more difficult to encourage people to participate and vote. Here are some things I have learned over the years that political campaigns can do to help increase voter turnout, even in local elections:

- Do not wait until Election Day to worry about turnout. Begin planning get-out-the-vote efforts at the start of the election campaign.
- Give voters something to vote *for*. As trite as this sounds, many voters do not vote because the candidates and the issues are not that appealing.
- When calling or visiting voters during the campaign, ask each voter to DO something—put up a sign or sign a petition. That way they will be more likely to remember and be part of the campaign.
- When asking people to volunteer, ask them to take Election Day off work, so they can be available to help turn out other voters throughout the day.
- Encourage people to vote by mail, or if your election allows, ask people to vote early. Voting early ensures that people do not forget to vote on Election Day.
- Remind people by mail and by phone that the election is coming up. You will be surprised how many people forget.
- When reminding people, ask them, "What time are you planning to vote?"
- Tell people where their polling place is. Polling places often change from election to election. This simple reminder is always appreciated.
- Try to have at least three Election Day volunteers per precinct whose jobs are to remind people to vote. One person can call voters, one person can visit voters, and one person can check the polls to see who still has not voted.
- Set high standards. Recruit people to volunteer *all day* Election Day.
- When calling do not take "I'm too busy or sick to vote" for an answer—it is an excuse. People are rarely too sick or too busy to vote. After all, voting only takes a few moments.
- There is no more important activity on Election Day than Get-Out-The-Vote. Everyone, including the candidate and all the campaign staff, should help.

- Keep working all the way up until the polls close.
- Treat **every** voter as though his or her single vote was the most important one. You never know, it could be.

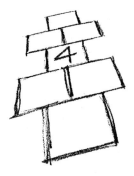

Sidewalk Strategy #4

Shut Up and Listen

When I was young, my father often told me, "Keep your mouth shut, you might learn something." It has taken me many years, but I have finally learned, as most kids do, that their parents' advice was right on target. In politics, as in life, you can learn a lot if you have the discipline to keep your mouth shut. Most people do not. Politicians rarely listen, and political consultants listen even less. Most people would rather be listened to than be told something, but political campaigns and politicians often make the mistake of trying to "educate" voters (telling them what they think they should know) rather than listening. If you do not listen, you miss opportunities to hear things that could help you. Accordingly, Chapter Twelve is about keeping your mouth shut.

Listening takes more effort than talking. Listening requires reflection and being open to new ideas. There are a variety of ways to listen to the public. The most effective takes the most effort: going door-to-door. Despite comments to the contrary, people appreciate it when someone takes the time to come to their door to talk, and I am always amazed at how much insightful information you can get if you make the effort. Is a street light needed? Has the neighborhood deteriorated or improved over the past several years? Why? Is traffic a concern? What suggestions do people have for neighborhood improvement? Not only do you gain valuable insight on issues of importance, you can also find people who are willing to volunteer or to help. Would you be willing to sign a petition for better streetlights? Would you be willing to volunteer to work on a neighborhood clean-up?

Chapter Thirteen discusses listening through public opinion polls which have become the preferred way for public agencies—for-profit and not-for-profit groups—public officials and those who aspire to be public officials to learn about community issues. Billions of dollars are spent every year on polls and public opinion research. Polls have many advantages over person-to-person work or door-to-door work: they are statistically accurate, they are quick, they are relatively easy to conduct, and they can cover wide geographic areas or targeted areas efficiently.

Chapter Fourteen is about listening through questionnaires. While not as statistically accurate as polls, written questionnaires, sent to a broad target of people, can also provide rich insight and valuable information. Questionnaires provide the intimacy of direct person-to-person contact while at the same time give an overview of the public's attitude toward various issues.

Whether you keep your mouth shut, poll or send out questionnaires, the important thing is to listen. Remember, a person would rather listen to himself than listen to you. "A bore," Ambrose Bierce, author of *The Devil's Dictionary,* wrote "is someone who talks when you wish him to listen." A good rule in politics: Do not be boring.

Chapter Twelve

Learn by Keeping Your Mouth Shut

One of the most important lessons I ever learned about listening was from one of the most powerful members of Congress, the late Phil Burton. At the time, Congressman Burton had served 19 years in Congress and was arguably one of the three most powerful elected officials in the country.

Burton had built a reputation as the person you *had* to have on your side to either pass or kill a piece of legislation. Unabashedly partisan, Burton is credited with numerous ground-breaking pieces of legislation. He authored the National Parks Recreation Act, the most sweeping environmental legislation ever passed by Congress. He wrote laws providing benefits to coal miners suffering from Black Lung Disease. He helped forge the coalition that banned oil drilling off the California coast. He was a steadfast champion for seniors, people with disabilities, working people and the poor.

Burton relished his role of power broker and counted among his friends and enemies the most powerful people in the country. He was used to barking out orders and telling people what he wanted—and he usually got it. When he called me and asked me to do a little research for him that required some door-to-door work, I was flattered and, of course, accepted, but not without serious reservations. Burton had a tough reputation and a stern demeanor.

Burton was in his first major political campaign in many years. Having lost a power battle in Congress by one vote to become house majority leader, he had re-channeled his unlimited energy as the Chair of Reapportionment for the Democratic Party. Burton had recently successfully crafted a blatantly partisan redistricting plan that gave Democrats the upper hand in many state and federal elections. To say his plan was creative was an understatement. He called it "my contribution to modern art." One district was described as looking like an "insect-like polygon with 385 sides." The result of Burton's creative redistricting allowed Democrats in California to win 60% of the Congressional seats despite Republican Ronald Reagan's landslide victory in the state.

Burton's partisan gerrymandering, while popular among Democratic office holders, was fodder for political commentators and editorial boards. They editorialized against him and attacked his partisan redistricting plan. Republicans, smelling blood, felt they had a chance to defeat their long-time nemesis. They recruited a popular San Francisco supervisor, Milton Marks, to run against Burton. Money was not a problem. The Republicans and their big business friends would spend whatever was necessary to win. Burton was worried. Had he gotten out of touch with his constituents? What were *real* voters thinking about him?

When I met with him at his San Francisco campaign office along with several other people he had asked to come, Burton explained what he wanted us to do. We were to walk door-to-door in several precincts and talk to voters about the election to get a read on what they were thinking. He was not totally comfortable with polls and wanted to hear directly from real voters. We were given lists of voters in certain targeted precincts, and we were instructed to note on our sheets the Burton supporters, the Marks supporters and the undecided voters. If voters had questions, we were to write their questions in the margins. Most important, we were to listen.

We were given our precinct lists and maps and were sent off. I was assigned a "mixed" neighborhood, made up of people who had lived in San Francisco for years as well as those who were new citizens and new arrivals to San Francisco. As instructed, I tried to "engage" people into conversation, to probe what they thought of Burton. I asked questions and jotted down their answers.

Some felt Burton had overstepped his power. Others said they thought the redistricting was wrong. Nevertheless, people recalled the good work he had done for the environment, for working people and for San Francisco. Despite some criticisms of him, their support was still strong. Many voters thanked me for coming by to talk to them and told me to thank Congressman Burton for listening.

After four or five hours of door-to-door work, I returned to the office—

the last of the people that Burton had sent out. Exhausted and tired, I was hopeful that I would drop my completed list in the mail slot of the headquarters and be on my way home.

When I arrived back at the headquarters, only Burton was there. It was late, and he was sitting at a table looking over the precinct lists others had turned in.

"Hey, thanks for your help today," Burton said, shaking my hand. "I bet you're hungry, aren't you? Can I get you something to eat?" This was the man who was known as a bully and who one time in a restaurant threatened a fist fight with Speaker of the House Tip O'Neill.

We sat down, and for 40 minutes, we went over the list of voters, name by name. "Tell me what they said to you," he asked. He wanted to know how I answered the voters' questions and what each person thought about him. I got the impression that he was already familiar with the neighborhood and the people in it. I expected he had walked the neighborhood before and was interested if attitudes had changed.

Nothing I said or learned during the precinct walk was particularly insightful or important, yet he listened to me as though what I had to say did in fact have importance.

When we were done, he thanked me again for sharing my time. He said he seriously appreciated my effort and help, and I believed him.

That was the last time I spoke with Congressman Burton. He died at 56 but not before trouncing his Republican opponent. The lessons I learned that day influenced the way I dealt with volunteers. I learned to treat volunteers with respect, to value their work and most importantly, to take the time to listen.

* * * * *

It took me a long time to learn to keep my mouth shut. In my early days of organizing, I talked too much and tried to answer questions before people asked them. It took me a long time to learn the art of keeping quiet and learning through listening. It took me a while to learn that you can often learn more from the question that is being asked than from the answer that is given. A person who asks a question just wants to be heard and is often less interested in the answer to his question.

I learned this lesson working with the largest public employees' union in

Photograph courtesy of Dennis Hearne Photography

The late Congressman Phil Burton and his wife, Sala Burton, celebrating re-election to the US Congress. Although one of the most powerful political leaders in the country, Burton made a point of listening to his local constituents.

San Francisco. The union was in danger of being "decertified" by its membership—essentially a death penalty for a union since it means workers are dissatisfied and would rather have no union than be represented by the one they had. To fend off the decertification vote, the union's leadership had hired me to direct their union staff in the hope I could help them convince people to keep the union.

I began by talking privately to each paid staff member of the union, some of whom had been part of the union staff for many years. I asked each one how often they visited the job sites. Most replied: "Only when a worker has a problem or a grievance."

I asked, "How often do you talk to the workers who don't have problems?"

"Why would we do that?" One staff member replied. "Our job is to help workers who have problems." Another staff person who had been with the union for many years said, "If we visited the job sites, we would be inundated with problems we could never solve."

I then asked, "Have you ever sat down and just listened to what the workers have to say? Have you ever asked them what they think of the union or what their problems are?"

"Never," the staff told me again and again.

In my experience, most people do not have "problems" on the job. Nevertheless, people without problems also are in need of union representation, and the union needs to be relevant to them, too, not just the workers with problems. I knew if we were going to fight off a de-certification vote, we needed to change the attitude of the union staff toward the workers—all of them.

Our first step in helping the union gain credibility was to learn more about the workers. To assist, I hired three organizers who had no prior experience working in this union but who were skilled organizers and were adept at listening and engaging people. Blending the new and the old staff, we began a "campaign of listening."

I instructed the staff to visit every floor in every building where the union had members and ask each worker what he or she thought of the union and what the union could do to be more relevant. I stressed to them: "Do not promise anything and do not, under any circumstances, try to explain or justify why the union hasn't done this or that. The workers are so full of anger against the union that they will never listen to anything you have to say until they have let out their anger. They need to vent before they can think about anything else."

I reminded them again, "Just listen to whatever they have to say, ask questions and listen some more."

One of the union staff members said, "What if someone says they are going to vote against the union? Shouldn't we try to talk them out of it?"

I explained, "If the union isn't doing its job, then there is no reason to have the union. Our job is to make the union relevant so workers will want the union. But first we need to know what *they* want, not what *we* want."

Our staff was advised not to try to talk people out of voting against de-certification. I told them, "The workers should be free to vote as they want. If we are successful fighting for issues they care about, they will support the union."

For five weeks, our staff went to hundreds of job sites. They kept detailed records of who they talked to, where people worked and what issues were important. The employees had plenty to say—none of it very good. Day after day, after spending hours listening to complaints that the union was terrible, that it "sucked" in their words, that it did nothing for them, the staff came back depressed. Many workers said this was the first time in years that they had ever seen a union staff member. Obviously, we had a big problem.

When we returned to speak to them again, many of the workers looked surprised to see us. As one employee told us, "We're amazed you are back. We didn't think you would want to come back again to listen to all our complaints."

Meanwhile, the staff wrote down whatever people said. If workers said the union was ineffective, our staff agreed but added that if it was going to be effective, the workers themselves had to make it better. We could help them, but the union could only be powerful if people became active in it.

Gradually, as a result of these conversations, we began to learn some important things about the problems the workers had been experiencing. Among other things, we learned that the city (their employer) owed *all* employees some back pay, which had been promised though the checks had never been issued. The workers blamed the union.

We also identified the real leaders at the different job sites and found that many of the union reps who attended union meetings were not the real leaders but people who had been "drafted" to go to union meetings. Most importantly, we learned that before we could get workers to listen to the union, the union had to listen to them. They had to feel that the union was really interested in learning about and addressing their concerns before they would take any steps to actively support it.

Since the most immediate concern was the back pay they had never received, echoed in complaint after complaint, we decided that our first campaign should be to go after the workers' back pay. Before doing so, the Union staff and I, now more knowledgeable, went back to the job sites and asked workers to be a part of the campaign to get the back pay. In some cases, we spoke to individuals one-on-one. In other cases, we asked the local worker leadership to set up a meeting where we could speak to the employees as a group.

Whether we spoke to people individually or in a group, our message was the same: The union does not merely *represent* workers—it *is* the workers. We told them that before we would go after their back pay, they would have to vote that this is what they wanted us to do. We printed ballots and asked each person to vote on whether or not this was a battle they wanted their union to take on.

The response of the workers was enthusiastic. No one from the union had approached them like this before, and now, they felt that the union really did want to listen. They voted overwhelmingly to support the campaign for back pay. They were eager to help, and we found many ways to involve them. We printed buttons saying: "BACK PAY NOW!" and distributed them to all employees. We organized delegations to visit the management demanding their back pay. We arranged for press conferences where we discussed the campaign for back pay and got workers to speak who described how difficult it had been for them to get the city to respond in the past and their economic difficulties due to this loss of pay. We distributed updates to everyone so they were kept informed about what was being done.

Within a few weeks, we won. Everyone received their back pay. To celebrate, we arranged ceremonies at each of the job sites acknowledging the work that people had done. We asked what had worked and listened to what the people said. One member of the union summed things up nicely when he said, "I never thought the union was relevant to me. Now, I've learned that by working together, we are more powerful. Thanks for listening to us."

A month later, when the vote to decertify the union was held, we won easily. The workers voted overwhelmingly to keep their union. The union had become relevant.

* * * * *

While it is possible to walk and chew gun at the same time, it is impossible to talk and listen at the same time.

In the California gubernatorial election of 2002, well over $100 *million* was spent by the Republican and Democratic candidates running for governor, but precious little of it was used to listen to voters or to the public. Both campaigns spent millions on TV ads talking about themselves or the shortcomings of their opponent. Phone calls (mostly recorded messages from celebrities) were made to voters, not to listen to them but to tell them how to vote. Mailboxes were stuffed with brochures that never asked but always told.

Candidates and their managers often resort to canned, over-used slogans to "package" themselves: "Tough on Crime," "Experience Counts," "Integrity and Ability," "New Energy." Rarely do they take the time to listen to voters. It is too bad, and it can cost you the election, as happened to my friend, Mayor Art Agnos in San Francisco.

Art had been elected mayor of San Francisco in 1987 and was finishing his third year in office. I had directed Art's field operation campaign during his first campaign for mayor, and Art was eager to duplicate our earlier success. Prior to getting his second campaign started, I asked a selected group of volunteers and former campaign workers to fan out across the city into various neighborhoods and ask people what city problem "bugged them most." The answer came back loud and clear—dirty streets ranked number one. I suggested to Art that we make cleaning the streets our focus for a few months and that he, as mayor, his volunteers and our campaign staff actually go out and sweep the streets in neighborhoods across the city, as a tangible as well as symbolic gesture. He immediately declined, telling me, "No way. Sweeping streets is beneath the mayor." I could not convince him. Instead, he wanted to focus on telling voters about all the great things he had accomplished in his first term.

Meanwhile, our opposition, I am sure, had also heard what we had heard from citizens. Several weeks after the mayor had rejected our idea of sweeping, our opponent and his supporters began sweeping the streets. The press loved it. The public loved it. Even though the election was some months away, the debate had been defined. Art's opponent, Frank Jordan, listened to the public and responded. Art was perceived as being aloof and more interested in telling voters what he did than responding to what they wanted done. On Election Day, voters swept Art Agnos out of office.

* * * * *

It takes a lot of discipline to keep your mouth shut, but new ideas and fresh perspectives are often a result, if you take the time to listen. A school district we worked with in the Silicon Valley had previously lost an election to generate funds to modernize the local schools. The common wisdom among board members and political insiders was the tax was too high and that senior citizens would not support any tax increase. I suggested that before they placed another measure on the ballot, they should send a questionnaire to seniors asking why they had not supported the last bond measure. The district agreed, and we sent 6,500 *hand addressed* letters to voters over 65 years old explaining the needs of the district and asking them to complete a short questionnaire. (The purpose of the hand addressing the letters was to increase our chances of the letters being read by those we sent them to).

To encourage a good response, we phoned every senior saying we valued their opinion and encouraged them to fill out the questionnaire. We received hundreds of responses, enough to fill two file boxes. Some mailed in the questionnaire, others wrote long letters, still others hand carried their completed questionnaire to the nearest school in their neighborhood.

We learned a lot just by asking. Some elderly voters complained that the schools needed painting, and on their own, volunteered to help paint. Others suggested that the district should appoint an independent oversight committee to review projects and expenditures.

The school district took the ideas that the seniors had provided and recruited people to help paint the schools and perform other tasks at well-publicized "School Clean-up Days." A district oversight committee was established. Volunteers, many of whom were senior citizens, joined the effort to fix the schools and to evaluate future needs of the schools. Less than a year later, the community overwhelmingly voted in favor of a new bond measure. It all started with listening.

Chapter Thirteen

Listen Through Public Opinion Polls

Since few politicians seem to listen to citizens, how do they learn what people care about? How do successful politicians seem to be so adept at creating campaign messages and themes that resonate with the majority of voters?

The answer is through polling.

For anyone running for office—from city council to the President—or for anyone wanting to pass or defeat a ballot measure, polls are a perceived necessity.

The influence of polling in political campaigns has been growing increasingly since the 1930's when George Gallup first developed the technique to measure public opinion. Conducted correctly, polls provide valuable information on how different groups of voters think or react to a candidate or issues. Polls are so much a part of our political process that if a consultant were to suggest managing a campaign without a poll, some campaign consultants would consider this malpractice.

Given the decline in personal contact with voters, polls are a necessity for anyone wanting to run for office or for any institution seeking the support of the public, and are an efficient and cost-effective way of learning about issues.

Candidates are not the only people to use polls.

It is a rare school district or governmental agency that will place a tax measure on the ballot without first conducting a poll to determine which projects voters are likely to support, what tax rate is acceptable and when is the optimal time to be on the ballot.

Polls are used by attorneys to help determine issues that will resonate with potential jurors.

The entertainment industry conducts polls to determine audience reaction to movies and TV shows—often changing scripts or endings based on their findings.

Newspapers use polls to measure reaction to current events and to determine what type of stories their readers want.

Businesses poll on everything from determining the public's taste in automobiles to toothpaste flavors.

Government agencies regularly poll citizens to determine support (or lack thereof) for various projects from building freeway extensions to reforming welfare.

While polling has become today's chosen method for elected officials to help make decisions or predict how the public will react, the concept of trying to predict the future is not a new one. In Ancient Egypt, the pharaohs looked to the advice of their high priests to help them keep an iron grip on the masses. These priests may have been the world's first political consultants, and they occupied powerful positions in Egyptian society.

Today, polls have replaced ancient methods of divining, and political consultants interpret these polls using a mix of science, magic, intuition and guesswork on behalf of eager politicians. Just as ancient political leaders would not go to battle or make other major decisions unless they had first consulted their oracles or advisors, so today, politicians and campaigners rarely wage political battles without consulting their polling advisors.

Because polls are so essential, pollsters, or "public opinion analysts," are commonly called into campaigns at the earliest possible moment to help guide the campaign and develop campaign themes. Most major decisions in a campaign are made based on poll results. The results are often treated as if they are sacred. One of the country's most successful political consultants prints only one copy of his survey results. Then, he binds the poll in a dark blue, hardback cover, which looks like an oversized Bible. The poll, like the word of God, is rarely challenged—only interpreted.

New technologies provide polling experts even more powerful and precise tools to understand how voters react to messages, both visual and verbal. For example, during the last presidential campaign, both major candidates used a technique to measure not only what people thought about issues but the importance of the candidate's body language and facial expressions on the voter. A representative group of preselected voters recorded their feelings on a computer *every ten seconds* while watching the presidential debate. Meanwhile, the researchers watched a video of these voters watching the debate and recorded their physical and mental reactions. By later analyzing the results from these three streams of information second-by-second, the campaign analysts were able to determine how those observed reacted to body language, facial expressions or humor. The results of this information was then fed to the candidates who modified and adjusted their speech patterns, use of humor and body language in an attempt to present a more likeable image.

The Down Side of Polls

While polling and new technologies provide valuable information to candidates and campaigns, there are down sides. Candidates rarely develop their own ideas forged from direct contact with voters, as they increasingly turn to polling to "hear" what voters are concerned about. Polls enable candidates and their campaign managers to shape their messages and image without even meeting with or talking to voters.

Polling has enabled politicians to become more and more isolated from the public, spending less time in direct contact with individual voters, than at any time in our nation's history. Public meetings today are rarely more than orchestrated "press events." Except in local elections, meeting personally with voters in their homes or at neighborhood gatherings has virtually become nonexistent.

Financial contributors often will not contribute money to a campaign unless there are positive poll results indicating the viability of a candidate or an issue. Poll results are important to create the impression that a campaign is gaining support. Reporters routinely ask campaigners, "What does your poll tell you?" and political campaigns orchestrate press briefings to put positive spins on poll results. Decisions on when to mail or when to advertise are often made with an eye on when the next poll will be conducted.

The greatest problem with polls is the reliance people place on them to accurately predict the future. While polls can provide valuable insight, they are not crystal balls. Polls measure public opinion at a specific point in time. For example, a poll done a week before September 11, 2001, would have very different results from one done after September 11.

The Importance of the Right Poll to the Correct Audience

The accuracy of a poll is determined by what questions you ask and who you choose to be a part of your polling sample. A polling sample for a political campaign must reflect who is likely to vote in a specific election. It must reflect the right percentages of men and women, ages, races and income levels. Determining which voters are likely to vote in a specific election and developing a polling sample from them is critical, but it is not always done correctly. If the sample of voters polled is not made up of voters who are likely to vote in a specific election, the results of the poll may not be accurate. It is essential to adapt the type of polling you do to the community and the election you are targeting.

I was speaking at the conference in South Africa on political organizing. I was due to give a presentation on mobilizing community support. Waiting for my turn, I listened to an American consultant speaking about the importance of polling.

About 300 organizers and activists were also listening intently and patiently to his presentation. When he finished his speech and asked for questions, a young South African raised his hand and asked: "Good sir, you have told us how polling works in your country. You have told us that the polling firm gets this important information by randomly calling voters and asking them questions. But, sir, with all due respect, how can we do that here in South Africa where the only people who have phones are the whites?"

For a moment, the consultant scratched his head, thinking of what to say and finally admitted, "Hmmm, I hadn't thought of that!"

Then, he went on, trying to encourage other questions. But while the audience members may have appreciated his honesty, they then regarded his comments with some suspicion. They continued to listen respectfully, but they did not ask further questions, and when he finished, they clapped politely but not with the longer and louder enthusiasm that greeted other speakers. By his answer, the polling consultant had shown he was unfamiliar with the conditions in South Africa, and this undermined the rest of his message, which was about how to apply the polling techniques of America to this new environment.

The most important question to answer when developing a poll is: "Who do I want to learn something from?" If you are running a campaign in a special election when turnout will be low, it is important to poll individuals who vote in almost every election. If you are trying to decide which election to put a ballot measure on, you might want to poll a wider target of voters—comparing how your measure will do in a low turnout election versus a higher turnout election. Who are you polling? All voters? Likely voters? People who never vote or who are not registered to vote? Establish your parameters based on whom you want information from.

You will also want to know what "subgroups" you want information from. Do you care how women look at the issue and whether their views differ from those of men? Are people who do not speak English a part of your target? If so, it is important to have interviewers who speak languages other than English developing a sample size sufficiently large to accurately measure opinions from this subset of people.

It has become increasingly popular for local candidates to use companies with national reputations to poll for local campaigns. While there may be some benefit to this, national firms often miss nuances or issues that are locally important but not nationally. In the November 2002 elections, many Democratic polling firms were widely criticized for encouraging Democratic candidates for congress and senate to focus on issues like prescription drugs and avoiding issues that did not poll as high nationally but were of concern to local voters. The Democratic losses in the elections were blamed, in part, on over reliance on advice from the national firms, who lacked the local perspective.

One of the biggest problems I have with polling is the over-emphasis people place on them. Elections have been won where poll results looked dismal and lost where polling indicated the election should be successful. Why? The most important reason is that polls cannot predict what the future will be nor can they measure the effect of hard work and smart strategy.

It is also possible to put too much importance on poll results, underestimating the importance of a campaign's ability to change public perceptions.

In the spring of 2002, Alameda Hospital in Alameda, California, was on the verge of closure. The hospital's revenue had not been keeping up with its operating costs, and the hospital was literally "running out of money." We were asked to help analyze whether the community would support a tax to keep the hospital open. The only hope for this 104-year-old institution to stay open to serve a community of 75,000 residents was to convince voters to support a tax of $298 per parcel, which would result in $6 million a year in new revenue for the hospital. While this tax, if passed, would be the highest ever for a hospital district in California, every penny was needed to keep the hospital functioning.

How successful would this vote be? Would voters support this hefty tax on their property? To find out, the hospital commissioned a poll to determine the likelihood of success. A 66.7% "yes" vote was required by state law, but the poll indicated that, at best, only 57% of the voters would support a tax, and less than 50% of voters would support a tax at the needed $298 rate.

The results of the poll looked grim, and the hospital had a choice to fold or fight. They fought. Though the poll numbers were discouraging and depressing, a group of hospital supporters, including doctors, nurses, senior citizens, hospital staff and patients, waged a campaign to encourage Alameda residents to vote "yes." To this end, over 70 volunteers phoned or walked the neighborhoods and rang the doorbells of every likely voter, explaining the issue and urging them to vote in favor of it.

The result? They won by garnering an unexpected 68.7% of the vote, despite a poll that had indicated no chance of success. By organizing volunteers and bringing their case to the voters who were most likely to vote on Election Day, the campaign was able to change the likely outcome that the poll had predicted.

When to Poll

Polls can only measure public opinion at a given point in time. After that, it is people and the effort they make that determines success. A successful campaign can and will change public opinion. Poll results are not set in stone and are accurate only at the time they are taken. Political reality is continually shifting, depending on the effectiveness of a campaign.

Polls are expensive. If money is an issue, when are critical decisions going to be made? While a candidate for a major office may poll as frequently as weekly, most campaigns are able to afford only one poll. If that is the case, it is important to decide when the information you will get is the most critical. An early poll may provide strategic insight and be helpful in creating themes and messages. A poll done closer to the election day may be helpful to identify who you need to get out to vote.

What to Poll

The real skill professional pollsters have is the ability to develop questions that are unbiased and not leading and providing thoughtful analysis once the poll is completed. Seemingly simple, the skill of developing questions is often well-worth the cost of hiring a professional polling firm. Polls are usually conducted on the phone and last no longer than 11 to 20 minutes. Care must be taken to determine exactly what you are attempting to learn. Do you want to know what issues voters care about? Do you want to know how your candidate would fare against various opponents? Do you want to know if your community will support a new tax, and if so, what tax rate is acceptable to voters? Do you want to know how voters and have voters rate city services? Before sitting down to write the poll, have a clear picture of what decisions you need to make and what information will be important.

Analyzing the poll can be simple or complex depending on your interest and skill. Most poll results that are reported in newspapers or on TV are normally called "top lines." Top lines provide a simple overview of what all voters think about an issue or candidate. More important is an analysis of what are called "cross tabs." Cross tabs allow the analyst to look at in-depth subsets of voters. What do African American women, ages 30 – 45 feel about an issue? What issues are important to seniors or newly registered voters? The degree of analysis is only limited by your imagination and the voter data available.

A Few Words of Caution

Polls are often used to manipulate public opinion. Unethical campaigns often call voters under the guise of a poll when the real purpose of the call is not to determine voter opinions but to persuade voters. "If you knew that 'candidate John Doe' was a convicted felon, would you be less likely to vote for him?" The truth may be that candidate John Doe had never been arrested or convicted for a crime, but the damage has been done under the cover of a poll.

In the public finance consulting industry, financial underwriters (who work with school and college districts, transit agencies, cities and counties) often do "free polls" and use the results in an attempt to convince public officials to place tax measures on the ballot. Public officials who are cautious about spending money on polling often rely on the industry-generated-and-paid for polls to make decisions. Often times, the district is convinced to put a poorly planned measure on the ballot rather than taking care to place a measure on the ballot that would better meet their long-term needs. These "free polls" are no more than marketing gimmicks to serve the interests of the financial advisors.

The growth and profitability of polling has encouraged many people to become "pollsters" without any specialized training or credentials. Some are able to conceal this fact behind misleading credentials. One successful pollster, who works in several states, promotes his Ph.D. in all his marketing, implying that he has studied the science of public opinion. The truth is that his Ph.D. has nothing do with statistics, psychology or polling. Others who grandiloquently call their firms "The Institute of …" or "The Center for the Study of …" are often merely one person operations managed by someone with a computer in the corner of their living room.

Another unscrupulous pollster was found to have hired professional actors to appear in a presentation he made at a state conference for school board members. The actors, who kept their identities and professions secret, were hired by the polling firm to give glowing testimonials about the accuracy and the utility of the polls conducted in "their communities." Unfortunately the conference leaders never learned of this ruse and many unsuspecting school districts were duped into hiring the dishonest firm.

Despite the few bad apples in the industry who prey on unsuspecting clients, polling will continue to be the most useful and accurate way to measure public sentiment. Polls provide a wealth of useful information about voters' views and what may motivate them to vote one way or another. But to fully benefit from a poll, you need to understand both the strengths of polling and its limitations. Here are some guidelines on what polling can and cannot do.

What Polls Can Do

- Polls can give you an understanding of the way voters think and feel, at a given moment, about candidates and issues.
- Polls can help determine issues and craft persuasive messages and themes.
- Polls can determine strengths and weaknesses of candidates and their opponents.
- Polls can help determine acceptable and unacceptable levels of taxes.
- Polls can help determine priorities of voters.
- Polls can measure how support has increased or decreased over time, thus measuring the effectiveness of messages or campaign strategies.
- Polls can help determine the opportune time to place a measure on the ballot.

What Polls Cannot Do

- Polls cannot predict exactly what the future *will be*. They can only give you an assessment of what that future *might be* if conditions remain unchanged. They cannot tell you what might happen in the future to change those conditions or how those changes will in turn affect the way voters think.

- Polls cannot measure the impact that the hard work of dedicated volunteers can make in a campaign. Polls cannot measure what is essentially immeasurable—how volunteers can influence people they talk to on the phone or who they meet as they go door-to-door.

- Polls cannot make tough decisions. Polls can provide added information. For example, a poll could suggest that a tax of $30 is acceptable to voters, and a tax of $60 is not; however, if the higher tax is needed to keep a hospital open or a program in a school funded, the poll cannot tell you what to do.

Polls, done properly, can provide information and insight well worth the cost. Knowing what messages are persuasive, knowing what to spend money on and what not to, is often well worth the cost of a poll; however, not every campaign needs a poll or can afford a poll. So what do you do if you are not able to afford the $15,000—$75,000 or more that polls cost? The answer: questionnaires.

Chapter Fourteen

Listen Through Questionnaires

Between the extremes of going door-to-door to find out what people are thinking and conducting an expensive poll, there are other ways to learn what people care about. I often use brief questionnaires, mailed or hand-delivered to voters, that simply and clearly ask their opinion on one or several issues. While direct mail solicitors are lucky to get a 3-5% return rate, we routinely get an astonishing 15-30% response rate to these questionnaires, even though we ask people to place their own postage on the reply card.

We have learned that, if asked, people are very willing to provide their opinions. A poll may provide a statistically accurate analysis of people's opinions, but questionnaires offer three advantages over polling:

First, they are sent to a broad target of voters, and the simple act of *asking people their opinion* may be as powerful or more powerful than the information actually gathered. People like the opportunity to give their opinion, and a questionnaire offers them that opportunity.

Second, questionnaires often provide more opportunity for qualitative input. The person who completes the questionnaire is able to add other information that is often helpful or insightful. For example, while a poll might provide an accurate overview of what the public feels about traffic, a questionnaire may reveal specific locations for a stop sign or speed bumps.

Finally, a person who takes the time to complete a questionnaire often may be recruited as a volunteer.

I recently ran a campaign for mayor in Berkeley, California. Our client, Tom Bates, the former Assembly member for the area, had been out of office for several years. In the first piece of mail to voters announcing his candidacy, we included a questionnaire and asked voters to rank the problems that concerned them most, from crime to fire safety to the quality of the local schools. We asked citizens if they were satisfied with city services and if they felt that the recycling programs were effective. We also left some space so they could tell us what other issues needed to be addressed in their city and in their neighborhood.

Hundreds of voters sent their completed questionnaires back to us. We heard from home owners and renters, senior citizens and college students. We had responses from people who lived in high-income areas as well as the less affluent parts of town. Some people attached long letters, articulating problems in their local neighborhood. We learned what streets needed to be repaired, and we heard about problems in the schools. Some people wanted to acknowledge the good work of some city employees, while others complained that some city employees were rude and condescending. Almost every letter was polite, although we did receive a few responses from the "outer fringe." One resident sent a letter full of deer feces and said that deer were ruining his landscaping.

The response was overwhelmingly positive. It gave us a sense of what issues concerned people in Berkeley, and if nothing else, a "to do" list for our candidate once he became mayor. In addition, a number of people volunteered to help on our campaign, and a few even sent in donations.

Every person who returned a questionnaire received a call from Tom, who thanked them personally for taking the time to write. (OK—he did not call the deer guy!). Imagine their surprise to get a call from the candidate for mayor saying he had read their note and wanted to thank them for taking the time to express their views.

The questionnaires gave us invaluable insight to the mood of voters and the issues they cared about without the expense of a poll. The simple fact that hundreds of people returned the questionnaire and took the time to write encouraged us to wage our campaign on "issues" and not the differences in the personalities of the candidates.

While it is obvious that a candidate should listen to his or her constituents, it is equally important for school districts and other public agencies to listen to the public, and questionnaires are an inexpensive but effective way of doing so. Throughout America, public agencies are dependent on voter

Please fill out and return this short survey…

1. What problems concern you most? *Rate each item using 1-5 • 1=biggest concern, 5=least concern*

- [ ] Education
- [ ] Affordable Housing
- [ ] Crime/Law Enforcement
- [ ] Business Opportunities
- [ ] Fire Safety and Preparedness
- [ ] Retail Shopping
- [ ] Traffic/Parking
- [ ] Other

2. Have you had a reason to contact the City of Berkeley in the past? If so, were you satisfied with the service you received?

3. Are you pleased with the fire and emergency services offered in your neighborhood? Do you have any ideas for improving emergency service?

4. Are you pleased with the job that City contra waste removal and recycling programs are doin

5. What other issues need to be addressed in y neighborhood?

Please provide the following information:

Name

Address

Phone

Email

- [ ] If you are interested in volunteering for my campaign, please check this box.

Let us know what you think!

COMMUNITY SAFETY SURVEY

Schools of Charleston County Facility Questionnaire

COMMUNITY SURVEY - How Would You Prioritize These Needs?

Cabrillo Community College Facility Questionnaire

Questionnaires are one of the many low cost, yet effective ways to communicate with voters and to learn what issues they care about.

support to improve facilities, approve budgets and provide additional revenue for programs. Public schools now contend for dollars in an even more competitive arena since they are up against private schools and charter schools in vying for students, support and money. They would find it easier to build community support if they did a better job of listening to the public. Transit agencies and library systems all need public support and tax dollars to improve services and programs. Regrettably, many public agencies do not listen to the public at all.

* * * * *

The problem of not listening enough became very clear when I visited a school district on the Central California coast. At a meeting with several school board members and district officials, the superintendent of schools for the district told me that they wanted to pass a $40 million bond measure that would, among other things, provide money to add new bleachers to the high school football stadium.

The mentioning of new bleachers raised red flags for me. Rarely are voters willing to pay for things they view as "nonessential," and sports facilities are often regarded as such. While I did not say it, I was concerned that the school district leaders may have been out of touch with their own community. I asked if they thought voters would approve a bond to improve athletic facilities, including bleachers.

"Well, of course, they will," one of the board members said, with great confidence. "On Friday nights, it's impossible to get a seat at the football games, and these games are the big social event for our entire town. Voters here might not support better classrooms, but they sure as hell support our football team!"

I was not so certain, but maybe this community was unique. I asked the superintendent to create a list of the most important projects that they needed money for, in addition to the new football stadium bleachers. I gave them a few days to review their needs, and when we talked again, they had prepared their list. Besides the bleachers, they listed a need for new science facilities, renovation of classrooms, the replacement of aging water and sewer lines and the expansion of the school library.

After reviewing the "needs list," I asked the members of the Board of Education if they would be willing to send a questionnaire to voters in the community asking them to rank in importance the various projects and the ones they would support if it meant a tax increase. The board members agreed, and we created a questionnaire listing all the proposed projects. We then sent a letter and a questionnaire to voters in the district describing these needs in further detail. We asked them to indicate the projects they would support if a bond measure were placed on the ballot, to rank those projects in order of priority and to return the questionnaire in a return envelope we provided.

We were pleased when over 20% of the people returned the questionnaire. We received responses from parents and non-parents, alumni and newcomers to the area. To the surprise of many, renovating the football bleachers not only ranked last, but many people (including parents) spontaneously added comments that if the school district put that project on the ballot, they would vote *no* against any school bond.

Though the bleacher project was dear to the hearts of many, the school district wisely kept it off the ballot. Instead, they placed on the ballot a bond that would pay for the cost of the most critically needed projects based on what the questionnaire had revealed. Instead of going down to an almost certain defeat, the school district ended up passing the first successful bond measure in the community in over 40 years.

Questionnaires provide a great way to keep in touch with voters, but keeping in touch with the community should not be limited to election time. The wise public official or public agency listens even when they do not need anything. It has been said that a good marriage is built upon listening to the other person and good communication. The same can be said of the relationship between an elected official or a public agency and the public. Listening and good communication are keys to a successful relationship.

The San Juan Unified School District, near Sacramento, routinely writes to voters updating them on how taxpayer money is being spent renovating the local schools. Often, they ask people to respond. The district recently sent a letter to voters updating them on the progress of the renovations in their local schools. The district received the following reply:

"I, for one, don't vote for bonds in relation to schools. I've said if the money would go to the repair of schools and not the bulk of it going to administration, I would vote. The letter I received today updating all the work done to these schools has really touched me. While I didn't vote for the last school bond measure, at last the schools are seeing the money. Please keep notifying the people of the good work you are doing. Thank you."

Listening is one of the lost arts of modern politics. Keep these things in mind if you do not have money to poll (and even if you do!):

People like to be asked their opinions on issues. Questionnaires and surveys can be a rich source of gathering information about the issues that concern them. Questionnaires can be sent in the mail or distributed door-to-door. The results from these questionnaires often provide keen insights that open the door for further contact. Someone who volunteers their opinion may be willing to volunteer their time.

When people take the time to complete a questionnaire, *you* should take the time to thank them for doing so. A simple "thank you" says to a person that they are important and that their opinion was listened to.

Follow up on issues people raise. If you ask people their opinion, follow up with them. Let them know their suggestion for a new traffic light is being looked into. If you asked about priorities for spending tax dollars— let them know that you listened to them.

Do not assume you know how the "community" feels about something. We tend to talk to people we agree with and who think like we do. To get reliable information, it is necessary to go outside of your circle of friends and acquaintances. School districts, for example, should make a point to communicate to nonparents. Unions should communicate to people who are not union members.

Keep in touch with voters, even when you are not asking them for something. Elected officials "reaching out" to voters spend vast sums of money during election periods. Many of these mailers get lost in the avalanche of mail that is sent out before Election Day. Communicate to voters when they are not expecting it or when you are not asking for something.

Sidewalk Strategy #5

Define the Debate

The most effective advertising commercials (the Marlboro Man, Nike's "Just do it!" and the American Express "Don't leave home without it") have been running virtually unchanged for years. Why? A simple message repeated again and again has a better chance of being remembered. You do not have to be selling cigarettes or sporting gear to understand the importance of a simple message. Candidates, school districts and even parents ("Do your homework!") need to have a simple message and the discipline to stay on it.

Chapter Fifteen deals with the challenges of developing a clear message that resonates with people and staying on the message long enough so it reaches people. Opposition, press, internal disputes and lack of resources all conspire to derail the campaign message. The winning campaign is usually the one that can define the debate on the terms it wants.

A clear message, repeated day-after-day, will eventually be heard. Chapter Sixteen, "Homeruns v. Singles," is about finding a message and sticking to it, even though it may not be the most popular theme or the theme that polled the best. In local elections—those for local offices and local ballot measures— finding a theme that resonates with local concerns is more important than a catchy slogan. Local campaigns are usually won by those who implement an effective campaign rather than those who have the catchiest slogans.

Most campaigns, whether they admit it or not, practice a form of discrimination. Renters are sent one piece of mail, homeowners another. Black or Hispanic voters often receive different messages than white voters. Chapter Seventeen is about stereotypes and how to avoid them. In local elections, distinctions and divisions built upon stereotypes are often incorrect. A successful campaign must reach across real and imagined differences among people to be successful.

No discussion of defining the debate would be complete without some discussion of the role of the press. Chapter Eighteen is entitled "Talk to people, not the press." While we do not advocate ignoring the press, we believe in local elections good press coverage, bad press coverage and no press coverage are about the same. In local elections, press reports about the campaign are far less important than the work the campaign does contacting voters.

Chapter Fifteen

Keep It Simple Stupid

Advertising students are often taught the principle of "K.I.S.S."—Keep It Simple Stupid. The idea behind this concept is that the attention span of people is short, and a simple message has a better chance of being remembered. During the Clinton/Bush Presidential Election in 1992, we all became aware of the necessity of keeping the message simple. In fact, James Carville, Clinton's campaign manager's mantra was "It's the Economy, Stupid!" Whenever Clinton or campaign workers got off message, Carville would bring them back to the theme that resonated with voters and could be explained simply and effectively, "Bill Clinton will get the economy moving."

Whether we like it or not, most people do not pay a lot of attention to politics. Concerns of putting food on the table, dealing with the kids, trying to make a living or coping with the hassles of commuting are higher priorities than following politics. Most people do not watch CNN, nor do they read the daily newspaper. Their lives are busy, and politics, no matter how important, is another hassle to them. At best, voters may spend only a few precious moments before they vote considering the merits of local candidates or issues. In politics, the simpler the message, repeated over and over, the better. A simple message usually wins over a complicated message. I know. I had to learn it the hard way.

Today, baseball fans in San Francisco crowd into Pac Bell (SBC) Ballpark to watch Barry Bonds chase baseball legends Hank Aaron and Babe Ruth for the all-time home run record. Each time Bonds hits a homerun into McCovey

Cove, the 40,000 plus fans in attendance who were lucky enough to get a ticket scream with joy. The Giants home ballpark is a baseball fan's dream. Built on the San Francisco Bay, it affords spectacular views of San Francisco and the Bay Bridge.

Many of the fans that crowd the park do not remember that the Giants failed four times on the ballot (twice in San Francisco, once in Santa Clara and once in San Jose) to get voter approval to build a new stadium. I was involved in two of the failed measures, San Francisco in 1989, which probably would have won if the Loma Prieta Earthquake had not hit the San Francisco area two weeks before Election Day, and Measure G in San Jose a couple of years later.

After "striking out" twice in San Francisco attempting to obtain voter approval, the Giants turned to San Jose with the hopes of convincing voters to support a new stadium. At the start of the campaign, everything looked positive. The mayor, the city council, the business community, organized labor and the newspapers all supported the measure. Our campaign was well-funded by business interests and the Giants. From both a financial and political perspective, we had everything we needed. City leaders were enthusiastic and supportive, and newspaper editorial writers and sports columnists wrote eloquently on the economic benefits of the ball park to the city of San Jose.

The campaign had more volunteers than we could handle. Who would not have wanted to volunteer and have the opportunity to mingle with Willie Mays, Willie McCovey, Orlando Cepeda and other Giant legends? Each Saturday, one or more of the baseball greats came to our campaign headquarters to speak to the volunteers and sign autographs. People came from far and wide to work on the campaign, and they were rewarded for their efforts by spending time with their heroes.

Money? We had plenty—enough to send numerous mailers to voters and absentee ballots to supporters. We gave away baseball caps, t-shirts, pennants, autographed baseballs and other trinkets as prizes to our volunteers. We called every voter and walked every precinct. Our opponents were out-spent, out-worked and out-organized. We lost.

We lost because our message was complicated, and our opponents' message was simple.

In our enthusiasm to convince voters to vote for the new ball park, which was to be paid for in part by a small increase in taxpayers' utility tax, we felt voters would be as enthusiastic as we were if they knew the "facts." We explained the economic benefits of the proposed ball park. We talked about the jobs that would be created by the new stadium and the increases in business activity and tourism to San Jose. We talked about intangible things like the national publicity that San Jose would receive as a "major league" city. We talked about the pleasure that a family could have taking their kids to the park on a warm summer night. We talked about summer jobs for youth and good clean fun. We sent mailer after mailer, some from Giants players, some from popular elected officials, touting the benefits of the proposed ball park to the city and residents of San Jose. We even sent voters a thick 42-page booklet of facts, including testimonials from local school superintendents and a detailed actuarial report on the economic benefits to the city.

One week before the election, voters received one piece of mail from our opponent. Jack Davis, a consultant from San Francisco, produced it and paid for it himself. The mailer was simple and brutally effective. It was a postcard in the shape of the life-sized face of the owner of the Giants, Bob Lurie, who had made millions in real estate. His ownership of the Giants was just one part of his considerable financial portfolio. In the post card, where Mr. Lurie's nose should have been, there was small cut out the size of a light switch.

The message: *Flip off Bob Lurie.*

The postcard stated:

Paste this over your light switch. Think of Bob Lurie every time you turn on your lights, cook a meal or heat a cold room. Bob Lurie is one of America's most wealthy individuals. In fact, Fortune 500 *has estimated his wealth to be almost $500,000,000 ... Mr. Lurie wants a new ball park so he can make even more money. That is his right. But is it right to pay for that ball park by taxing everyday essentials? Think of Bob Lurie every time you turn on your lights, cook a meal or heat a cold room!"*

A simple message, dramatic and effective—and it killed San Jose's chance for major league baseball.

* * * * *

The simpler the message, the better. It has been estimated that most voters spend just a few moments reading campaign mail and perhaps a few seconds listening to a campaign ad. Many voters make decisions on who and what they are going to vote on with little research or much thought. It stands to reason that the simpler the message, the easier it will be for a voter to

144

remember the key elements. Few voters read campaign mail from front to back. The message needs to be simple and effective if it is going to be read before it hits the garbage can or the recycling bin.

A city council candidate we worked with had failed in a previous attempt at elective office. Despite outspending his opponent, he failed to "connect" with voters and lost to an incumbent that had been in office for over 24 years. Undaunted by this defeat, he moved into a new district and hired us. His new opponent was a well-known community activist who had been involved in many community issues over the years and had wide support from the community and political leaders.

To get started, we drove together through the district to get a feel of the neighborhoods. This simple drive through the neighborhoods revealed many things. Streets were filthy, schools were run down, drug dealers sold drugs openly on the streets and the commercial areas had abandoned buildings. Groups of unemployed young men loitered around liquor stores. While there were no shortage of issues or needs to communicate with voters, voters in this district had a lot of things on their minds, and who they were going to elect to city council was not one of them.

Our strategy to win the election was simple. Every Saturday and Sunday, the candidate, his wife and kids, their friends and any supporters or volunteers we could recruit would sweep the streets of the district. Armed with brooms, shovels and garbage bags, our goal was to clean every single street in the district.

I explained to my client, "People in this district may be poor, but they are smart. They will recognize bullshit when they hear it. If you tell them you are going to fix the schools, get the drug dealers out, bring new business into the community, they will either laugh at you or ignore you. They know better. They know how hard it is to do that. Do something that you can do. Let's show voters that you are a person that gets things done. Once you are elected, you will have the power to do bigger things."

Although the candidate was less than enthusiastic about sweeping streets every week, to his credit, he swept with us. For two months, like clockwork every Saturday and Sunday, we swept, dressed in bright yellow T-shirts emblazoned with our candidate's name.

We also mailed a letter to every voter before we swept a neighborhood asking people to help us. During the "sweeps," we distributed leaflets door-

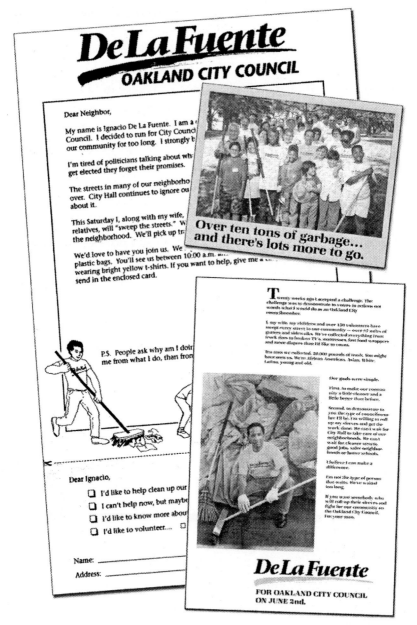

Our strategy to win the election was simple. Every Saturday and Sunday the candidate, his wife and kids, their friends, and any supporters or volunteers we could recruit would sweep the streets of the district. Armed with brooms, shovels and garbage bags, our goal was to clean every single street in the district.

to-door asking the residents to join us. Each week, more people joined us. When we completed sweeping a neighborhood, we sent another piece of mail, just in case they missed us. When residents saw us, some came out of their houses to help, while others brought sodas or water. Many brought their own brooms and joined the effort. In everything we did, we stayed on our message: "Our candidate is the guy who cleaned our streets."

It was not easy, neither the work nor keeping focused on the simple message. Sweeping streets every Saturday and Sunday is not what candidates envision doing when they run for office. Each week, the candidate said: "When can I talk about issues?"

Our response: "The only issue is clean streets. If we can demonstrate we can do that, maybe, just maybe, voters will trust you to do something else."

Our opponent was a good guy and a good candidate. He wrote thoughtful position papers and he had endorsements of key people. He attended every candidate night and every forum. He sent voters well thought-out positions on a variety of issues.

The election was not even close. Our candidate won in a landslide. On Election Night, we were joined by hundreds of volunteers, many who we had met on the sweeps. Raising brooms over our heads, we celebrated our victory.

* * * * *

We often work with school districts that need voter approval of tax measures to fix buildings or build new schools. We tell them all the time, "Keep your message simple. Voters don't care about all your needs, they have many other things to think about.

"If you need to repair and renovate schools, tell them *that*. Tell them that again and again and again."

Public agencies, whether they are schools, hospitals or cities and counties have a difficult time communicating effectively to voters. They often think more words are better or that voters actually watch the televised city council or school board meetings. Educators often speak in what we like to call "eduspeak," a language that only educators understand.

Here is an example:

"The HVAC systems in our technology center have ceased to provide adequate circulation to our students. In addition, there is a shortage of adequate instructional facilities and infrastructure."

Translation: "The school is overcrowded, and the heaters and air conditioners in the science lab are broken."

The simpler the message, the more likely it will be remembered and the more effective the campaign.

Politics is not the only arena where simplicity and repetition of message is important. Advertisers repeat commercials again and again. Nike's "Just do it!" has become part of our language. "Got Milk?" while not as ubiquitous as "Just do it!" has helped the milk industry bring contemporary style to a common product thousands of years old.

After I left the UFW, I was asked by California's Superintendent of Public Instruction to see if I could identify ways to increase parental involvement through organizing to help improve academic performance in inner city/ lower achieving schools. Working with teachers and principals in some of the toughest neighborhoods of East and West Oakland, we developed some strategies that dramatically increased test scores in reading.

The core of our plan was to encourage parents to spend 10–15 minutes a night, every night, reading to their children. While the concept was not new or unique, we approached our plan as a campaign, and we used every technique at our disposal to "educate" and encourage parents and other family members to read with their children.

We started by sending personal letters (in 15 different languages) to every parent or guardian in our targeted schools. The letter stated how important reading was to children, and even if children were too young themselves to read, a parent could read to them. In the letters, we provided practical tips to encourage reading:

- Turn off the TV.
- Read to your child every night.
- Find a quiet, well-lit place for your child to study or read.

Next, we got the kids involved. We asked them to ask their parents to read to them every night, and we asked the kids to ask their parents to "Sign a Pledge" saying they would. Each child that brought to school a signed pledge—it could be signed by a parent, a grandparent or even an older sibling— was praised. Our goal was to achieve 100% participation in every class.

While we got the kids involved, we kept communicating to the children's families. We sent first class letters to parents. We sent a large 17 x 24 inch piece of paper with the words "Tape this over the TV" to encourage people

Design courtesy of Jane Norling Designs

Sometimes, the fewer words the better. This simple poster was the cornerstone of a campaign to pass a $200 million bond measure to clean up Lake Merritt in Oakland, to restore urban creeks and to improve parkland. The Measure passed with 80% support.

to turn off TVs and start reading. We printed up colorful cardboard "campaign signs" that boldly proclaimed: "Reading is Fun!" We went door-to-door in the community and asked everyone, not just families with school-aged children, to put the signs in their windows.

We organized marches on Saturday where we walked through the neighborhood with kids and parents holding signs that said: "We read!" "Reading is Fun!" "Take ten minutes a day to *read* to your child."

We organized phone banks and called each home, thanking every family for spending time reading. Principals and teachers found books to share, and each child was given a book of their choosing.

For six months, we kept emphasizing our theme that reading was fun. In the end, when the state released test scores, we were not surprised that test scores in reading for all our targeted schools had risen.

Our simple message, repeated again and again, had gotten through. Reading was fun.

When communicating with the public, follow these two simple rules:

Rule one: The fewer words you use, the better.

Rule two: Develop a clear message, then stay on it.

A simple message repeated again and again will have a greater chance of being remembered than a message that changes all the time. But just as important as the message is the careful implementation of campaign strategy. It is a slow, steady accumulation of support over time that succeeds most often. While it is the big home runs that are remembered, a steady accumulation of "singles" usually wins the games.

Chapter Sixteen

Homeruns v. Singles

Campaign consultants are always looking to hit a "home run." In politics, a home run is defined as a significant issue that could sink an opponent or, conversely, propel a candidate or issue to victory. An example of a home run would be the discovery of someone cheating on their income tax or lying about where they graduated from college or degrees earned. Jack Davis' "light switch" about Bob Lurie was an example of a home run.

We once found out that an opponent of our client for city council had lied about her education. She had, on numerous occasions, touted her degree from a top Eastern women's college. She listed her BA and educational credentials in all her campaign literature and her campaign web site. When we checked with the college admissions office, we found that she had never graduated from this college. We promptly made her honesty an issue in our campaign, and she lost. Honesty and truthfulness became the issue. That was a home run.

A significant percentage of campaign resources are often spent on research to uncover an opponent's weaknesses, or to look for that "home run" or one issue or one character flaw that will make voters reject the candidate. The term for this is "opposition research." Anything the candidate has done in his or her life is fair game, from small issues to more significant ones.

- Did he vote in every election that he was eligible to vote in?
- Who has she accepted money from?
- Are there any nasty records from a divorce or a business?
- Was he ever a member of a controversial organization?

- Did she pay back student loans?
- Did he drink or smoke marijuana or has he ever been arrested?
- What organizations does she contribute money to or is a member of?

The list is endless. The more "important" the election, the more likely opposition research will be used and the more likely that negative campaigning will play a part. Bob Mulholland, a consultant to the Democratic Party in California, defends the use of negative campaigning saying that voters only remember the negative, not the positive. Negative campaigning has been part of American politics since the founding of the country. Usually, those who complain most about "negative" campaigning are those on the other side of the political fence. I usually think my opponents mail is negative, and the mail we produce is "issue based," while our opponents probably think our mail is negative, and theirs is factual. What is perceived as negative is often based on one's perspective.

The press is fascinated with negative campaigning. While editorial boards rail against negative ads and mudslinging, their reporters regularly call our campaigns wanting the dirt (on or off the record) on our opponent. Negative campaigning often helps to delineate issues and creates dividing lines along which comparisons can be drawn and decisions made. Negative campaigning separates fact from fiction and can help bring exaggerating politicians down to earth. The simple truth is campaigns engage in negative campaigning because it works.

Political consultants work hard to create an image of being tough and ruthless. Former Clinton advisors, James Carville and Dick Morris, have signed lucrative book and TV deals by marketing not only their political savvy but also their ruthlessness. Home runs sell.

One of this country's most successful political consultants admitted to me that he was always looking for the "home run" in a campaign. So what if he "struck out" occasionally and his candidate lost, he was building a reputation as a "no holds barred" consultant who it would be better to have on your side than against you. As he told me, "No one remembers who the top singles hitters are, but everyone knows the names of the top home run hitters. If you want to make a reputation in this business, your opponents have to fear you." He went on, "Half of my clients hire me because they don't want me to work against them."

Over the many years I have been working in politics and organizing, I have observed that the people who are successful are not those who have the best ideas or are the most ruthless or those who produce the most beautiful campaign brochures or TV ads but, rather, the people who work the hardest. The candidates who are willing to walk door-to-door everyday usually triumph over the ones who will not. The campaign that is able to recruit enough people to make personal calls to voters usually beats a campaign that relies on "paid phoners" or pre-recorded calls. Visit a campaign office in the evening or on a weekend day, the successful campaign will most often be bustling until late at night, while the unsuccessful campaign's doors are closed at 5 P.M.

Local campaigns are usually won by implementing a thoughtful strategy in a methodical and seamless manner, not by swinging for the fences. In fact, some of the same baseball language could be used to describe attributes needed to win at the local level:

Sacrifice. Teamwork. Solid fundamentals. Effort.

In a campaign for mayor in a large city, we went head-to-head with "Mr. Home Run," who was running the incumbent mayor's campaign. After extensive polling, the incumbent mayor and his consultant discovered crime was the biggest problem in the city. The police union, the local chamber of commerce, the business community and virtually all members of the city council supported the mayor's re-election. My candidate was a librarian who had recently been elected to the city council and who was supported by neighborhood activists.

While the incumbent mayor put out a glossy brochure touting his record against crime, our campaign went door-to-door and talked to voters. While crime was on the minds of voters, we also discovered that the local garbage company had recently raised its garbage rates and that garbage service was poor. Cans were not being picked up, drivers were discourteous and complaints went unanswered. The mayor had voted for the rate increases, and the garbage company was one of his biggest financial contributors.

We put out a mailer comparing garbage rates in this city with neighboring cities, and we asked people their opinion regarding their garbage service. We asked voters to complete a survey rating their local garbage service and to send the completed survey back to us.

We received thousands of responses, many of which included handwritten notes saying things like:

"Thanks for raising this issue."

"I've been complaining about garbage service for years, finally someone listened."

PETITION TO LOWER GARBAGE RATES

We the undersigned residents of Richmond are angry.

In the last year our garbage rates have skyrocketed from $12.00 per month to almost $20.00 per month.

Despite opposition by citizens, the Mayor and City Council recently approved these rate increases which give Richmond Sanitary Service a *guaranteed profit of 12% plus an unjustified cost of living increase!*

While all residents are paying for "backyard service," many of us haul our cans to the street. If we are paying for backyard service why don't we get it?

WE SUPPORT COUNCILMEMBER ROSEMARY CORBIN'S EFFORT TO LOWER GARBAGE RATES

WE WANT Richmond Sanitary to roll back rates to Richmond residents comparable to that which Richmond Sanitary charges Hercules and Pinole customers (Hercules $14.52 per can per month and Pinole $14.75 per can per month).

WE WANT Richmond Sanitary to offer a rebate to all customers who are paying for backyard service but are not receiving it.

NAME PLEASE PRINT	ADDRESS	PHONE
Kate Smith	120 Crest Richmond, CA 95814	555-1212
1.		
2.		
3.		
4.		
5.		
6.		
7.		
8.		

RETURN TO COUNCILMEMBER ROSEMARY CORBIN
114 CREST AVE., RICHMOND, CA 94801

Polls sometimes miss important issues. While our opponent campaigned on "crime," we campaigned on reducing garbage rates—and won!

"Best of luck."

"Let me know how I can help."

We also heard about other issues that concerned residents: lack of streetlights, streets that needed to be repaired and the need for crossing guards around schools. We heard from home owners who had complained to no avail about homes being built on unstable hillsides. Yes, we heard about crime, but there were other issues that could be addressed, and we learned about them. There were no home runs here to hit, only issues that voters cared about, and they thought a mayor should solve.

Among City Hall and political insiders, our candidate was snickered at. We heard later that "Mr. Home Run" gloated that the incumbent mayor would win in a landslide. Crime was the number one concern of voters in the polls, and we were ignoring it.

Meanwhile, we kept walking the neighborhoods. People thanked us for raising the "garbage issue" and wished us good luck. The incumbent mayor continued to send out one great looking brochure after another. TV spots were added to his arsenal. He appeared with police who said that he was tough on crime.

Our campaign attracted volunteers who had never been involved in a political campaign before. Many of them were the people we had met door-to-door or who had sent in a survey to us about a neighborhood concern. All through Election Day, these volunteers worked on the campaign, calling and walking neighborhoods, reminding their neighbors to vote. In contrast, the incumbent mayor on Election Day hired people to drive around the city in cars mounted with loud speakers urging people to vote for the mayor who is "Tough on Crime."

To the surprise of everyone in our opponent's camp, and no one in ours, we won. We won because we implemented a strategy that respected voters' intelligence and their desire to elect, not an image of a mayor but someone whom they believed could solve problems. There were no home runs for us, only singles. Every day, we kept at it. Every voter in the community was visited, and over time, we recruited others to help us, many of whom walked their own neighborhoods. They became part of our team.

* * * * *

In the summer of 2002, we had a kick off meeting for Tom Bates, who was running for mayor of Berkeley, California. We were as prepared as we could be, or so we thought, to handle the 100 or so people we had recruited to come and walk precincts on behalf of Tom.

The campaign headquarters was painted with a large sign supporting our candidate. One wall was painted blue so we could put up gold stars with the names of people who had volunteered (blue and gold are the colors of the University of California in Berkeley). Drinks and coffee were ready. Bagels and cream cheese were there for those who wanted them. We prepared packets of materials for walking, including maps and lists of voters arranged by street address.

The meeting started well enough. Tom spoke eloquently, as did others. We gave people instructions on going door-to-door and had a brief "role play" to instruct people how to answer voters questions. Unfortunately, before we dispatched people, one person in the front stood up and asked, "Is this coffee 'fair trade' coffee? We shouldn't be drinking coffee that isn't 'fair trade' coffee!"

Before we could answer another said, "Why are there Styrofoam cups here, don't you know they aren't biodegradable?"

A third said, "I oppose the use of yellow stars. Jews had to wear yellow stars in Nazi Germany."

Other questions rang out. Some said it was too early to walk, others said it was too late. It was clear that at least some of our "volunteers" wanted to talk more than they wanted to walk. A few, not interested in walking precincts, thought the election would be won if our candidate issued thick position papers on everything from panhandling to global warming. These were the old time "activists," people who Cesar Chavez liked to describe as armchair liberals—people more comfortable talking about the state of the world rather than working to improve it. At least 20 potential volunteers left, some muttering to themselves that Berkeley never changes.

It is a lot easier to debate the state of the world or the state of the city than to work to make it better. The simple truth is that if you want to win a local election, it is better to have 15 volunteers who are willing to walk precincts than 100 people who want to sit in the campaign office and debate strategy.

If you want to be successful organizing:
- Listen to the people who do the work, not the people who offer advice.

- Understand that an observation from someone who has walked a precinct is more valuable than the comments of someone who has attended a fundraiser.
- Believe that there are no shortcuts to successful organizing. Those that work usually win. Those that talk usually talk.

In local elections, effort and solid fundamentals usually triumph over short cuts. Success is more often due to making small incremental progress than by a dramatic event. Gimmicks do not win elections or organize people. The truth is the people who win elections, by and large, work harder and smarter than the people who do not. Many people equate talking to working. Unfortunately, they are not the same.

Politics breeds and attracts know-it-alls and pseudo-experts. In every community, you will find the experts who will freely provide their political advice and wisdom gained through years of talking to their insider friends. Most of the advice is useless, and people who often freely dispense advice rarely work hard doing the small things it takes to win elections. While I have no statistics to prove it, I would bet that more elections are lost from internal problems than obstacles or challenges from the opposition.

Chapter Seventeen

Avoid Stereotypes

Technology has forever changed the way political campaigns are run. Today, anyone with basic computer skills using voter data available from the county clerk or the Registrar of Voters can determine who is likely to vote in a particular election and who is not. Technology also provides the consultant with the ability to target groups of people based on assumptions and research about how people who share demographic traits may react to certain messages.

Despite the many advantages sophisticated technology can provide to campaigns and organizers, there is not one campaign that we are involved in that I do not worry that by using our sophisticated tools to target, analyze and segment voters, we are in fact hurting the democratic process. We often assume certain classifications of voters think one way and our messages to them perpetuate stereotypes. New technologies allow campaigns to target various subsets of voters and to ignore others.

Democratic women often receive different mail than their Democratic male counterparts, while Republican women may receive another message, and Republican males over 50 yet another. It is possible that an older voter receives only information about social security, while younger voters may only receive information about the environment, and young couples only information about education. Renters may receive one piece of mail, home owners yet another. Parents are assumed to support education, and senior citizens are assumed to be against tax increases.

By using easily available voter files, one can identify unlimited combinations of voters and send targeted messages to these subsets of voters. Here are just a few examples of the infinite classifications of voters that are publicly available:

- single Asian women, 25-35, who vote only in presidential elections
- older Italian American men who are Democrats and live in certain zip codes
- Hispanic voters who are renters, living in a household with a voter who is not Hispanic.
- home owners, 40-65 years old, who vote absentee and who purchased homes over 20 years ago
- voters who are newly registered but never have voted
- senior Republicans living in rental units
- voters who only vote in local elections

The possibilities are virtually endless, and by blending polling information, census data and tax assessor information, it is possible to classify voters based on even more demographic variables, and then use this information, to identify various issues and themes that may resonate with the different subsets of voters.

The benefits of this sophisticated targeting and categorizing of voters are significant. Campaigns are able to spend precious money and time communicating to specific voters who are most likely to support a particular position and who are likely to vote. Since the costs of direct mail and advertising are so high, it is necessary to make smart decisions on where to spend limited campaign dollars. Excluding people who are not likely to vote can help reduce expenses, as can not mailing or calling individuals who are already very likely to oppose a position or candidate.

I became keenly aware of the limitations of targeting while watching my 70-year-old father react to political mailings. He routinely threw away political mail that began "Dear Senior Citizen." Usually, these mailers were trying to scare him about social security or some other "senior citizen issue." Despite his age, these were not his issues. As he told me: "Just because I am 70 years old doesn't mean I don't care about education or the environment!" Once, even more critically, he complained about one such flyer: "Who writes this horse manure? Some 20-year-old who thinks he knows how someone 70 years old thinks!" He was right on.

When I find myself thinking I know how a certain "group " of people may think, I remember a lesson I had years ago as a white organizer assigned to a black community to build support for what was perceived as a Mexican union.

* * * * *

I had been working with Cesar Chavez and the United Farm Workers for about 4 years in California. The UFW had recently signed a union contract for Florida citrus workers who worked for Coca-Cola, which owned Minute Maid Orange Juice. The new union contract provided these Florida workers better wages, benefits and working conditions.

With four years of organizing under my belt, I was (unbelievably) one of the more experienced union staff members, and I was given the assignment to travel to Florida to build more support for the Union. I remember sitting in Cesar's office when he told me to go to Florida. While proud to be asked, I had a lot of questions: *Where would we live? What support existed there already? Why did Cesar think I could do it?*

After a while, I asked the real question on my mind. *How could I, as a white organizer, be effective in a black or Cuban community?* Cesar replied: "People will see what is in your heart. If you are good, you will be successful. People are color-blind when they experience good organizing. You'll do fine." I was less sure, but I kept quiet.

Three of us—my wife Ann and I, and our 1-year-old daughter, Jennifer— headed off to Florida in my Datsun pickup truck, packed with our few worldly possessions in the back. After a five-day drive across the United States, we found our way to Avon Park in Central Florida, where I had the name and address of Mack Lyons, the director of the union office in Avon Park.

As we approached the town, we passed orange groves that stretched for miles, and our noses burned with the smell of phosphates and fertilizers in the thick humid air. We drove through swarms of insects the locals called "love bugs," and more than once, we had to stop to scrape the squashed bugs off our windshield in order to see.

As in other small towns in the South, there was a "good side" of the tracks and a "wrong side." The address we were looking for was clearly on the "wrong side." The simple unpainted wood homes were perched up off the ground on short stilts. It was late in the day, yet it was still muggy and hot, and people were sitting on their porches while their kids were playing in the rutted dirt streets.

Looking for the address, we noticed a house where the distinctive black eagle UFW flag was hanging. I decided to ask for directions. So I parked, got out of the truck and knocked on the door. I expected to see a Hispanic family—who else, I thought, would have the union's black eagle flag displayed?—but the man who opened the door was not Hispanic. He was African-American, as was everyone else in the neighborhood. Even so, he, like many others we were to learn, proudly displayed the Union flag in front of their homes.

I concealed my surprise, however, and simply asked, "Do you know where Mack Lyons lives?"

"Sure do. But he's at the union office. You're real close," he said and then added, "You must be from California." He motioned towards my truck, where he could see the license plate. Then, stepping out on the porch, he commented, "Welcome to Avon Park, brother. Now follow me, and I'll take you to our union office." He got into his beat up Ford pickup, and we followed.

I mentioned to Ann how strange it was to see the Union's flag in the homes of black workers. For me, the Hispanic-UFW association was a powerful one since the Union had become a symbol of *La Causa*. A striking black eagle insignia had been chosen by Cesar to represent the Union. Throughout the Southwest, Mexican-Americans (farm workers as well as non-farm workers) proudly wore buttons with the black eagle as a symbol of their support for the union and as a symbol of pride in their own Mexican heritage.

The Union office was in a small, wood-frame, one story building and it was filled with several dozen workers—all African-Americans—who were there for a union meeting. Ann, Jennifer and I were the only white faces there. The man who led us there took us over to Mack, who welcomed us and introduced us to the whole group. To a person they greeted us warmly and thanked us for coming from California.

One of the women took Jennifer and sat and rocked her, and Ann and I were given iced tea to drink.

As the meeting came to an end, one of the workers stepped up to the front and led everyone in singing a spiritual followed by "We Shall Overcome." We all joined hands and sang.

That evening, we all went out to dinner at a small restaurant in the

Photo credit: Walter P. Reuther Library, Wayne State University

In Florida, the black eagle had come to symbolize the plight not just of Hispanic farm workers in California and the Southwest, but of exploited farm workers everywhere.

community. I told the story of stopping to get directions and expecting to see a Hispanic face because of the flag. Several of the workers laughed saying that people from California usually made that same mistake. They explained that in Florida the black eagle had come to symbolize not just the plight of the Hispanic farm workers in California and the Southwest but exploited farm workers everywhere.

In that small town in Central Florida, my own stereotypes were challenged and replaced by a new, broader understanding of what the fight for the farm workers and their black eagle symbol was all about.

* * * * *

Minority voters are particularly vulnerable to stereotyping. Campaign mail to African-American voters often features the image of Martin Luther King, Jr., as if these voters are so influenced by Dr. King that they will blindly vote one way or another because they see his picture on a brochure.

Discrimination is illegal, but stereotyping is not, although it can be just as harmful. In many ways, popular culture—television, videos and movies—perpetuate racial and ethnic stereotypes. The media tells us how "soccer moms" think, and it paints superficial portraits of African-American youth as well as people who live in rural America. A successful organizer treats people as individuals, not as members of a group.

Here is a radical observation: Minority voters care about the same issues that non-minority voters care about—good schools, healthy communities, clean air, efficient government and reducing traffic—and efforts to create special mailings or messages to minority voters are essentially viewed by them as transparent and patronizing.

Most of our clients for elective office are minorities. Our success rate is over 90%. Our "secret formula" for winning isn't really very secret. We make sure we work harder than our opponent and we never target voters by race. We treat very voter as we would like to be treated – as an individual with his or her own mind and opinions.

Today, one of our most successful clients is Wilma Chan. Wilma is a first generation Chinese American and has become one of the most powerful and effective legislators in California. When I first met Wilma she was running for election to the Board of Education, and I was running the campaign of her opponent. As I heard Wilma speak at various events during that campaign I was impressed with her knowledge of children's issues and her commitment to improve educational opportunities for all children. The election was one of the first we ever lost and it was due to Wilma's hard work. She walked every neighborhood, spoke to every voter and in the end, voters – of all races – voted to elect her to office.

Four years later, Wilma contacted us to run her campaign for the County Board of Supervisors, and while it was not possible to walk every precinct or talk to every voter personally, we ran a campaign that asked voters their opinions on issues. Wilma ran her race not as a Chinese-American candidate, not as a female candidate, but as a person who could effectively represent *all* citizens in the district. She won that race and went on to become Assembly Majority Leader, one of the most powerful elected officials in California.

* * * * *

Senior voters can also be victims of stereotyping. In 1998, I ran a tax election for the Beaumont Unified School District in Beaumont, California. Beaumont is known for two things: an amazing number of resale and antiques shops that line the main streets and a large conservative senior citizen population who live in several large retirement community complexes within the city limits. Many of these seniors moved to Beaumont from other parts of the country to take advantage of the warmer climate in Southern California. Since 60% of the registered voters were over 65 years old, the common wisdom was that it would be foolhardy to attempt to pass any new tax especially one that required two-thirds voter support. Voters in Beaumont are known for being frugal with their money. No tax election had passed in many years. Most elected officials, the local newspaper and local civic leaders were pessimistic about our chances.

To make matters worse, from our perspective, parents with children in the schools made up less than 10% of the registered voters, fewer still were likely voters. The schools were in terrible shape, temporary portable classrooms had been added to relieve overcrowding, and original school buildings, built years earlier, needed significant repairs. The school district had no funds to make the needed repairs. If the schools were going to be fixed, it would be necessary to ask voters to increase their taxes and vote for a bond measure.

Some leaders in the community said it was crazy to put a measure on the ballot. We had no choice but to ask senior citizens for their help. Without support from the "senior community," we had no chance of winning. Reaching out to and involving seniors in our campaign was not window dressing, it was critical to succeeding.

Rather than "writing off" seniors or avoiding them, we reached out to them and spent time answering their probing questions. We explained how much the new tax was going to cost them (for most, less than $20 per year). We asked if they had grandchildren and explained that the renovations in the schools would provide children (like their own grandchildren) better and safer opportunities.

We recruited one senior citizen to be our fund raising coordinator, another to be our office manager and yet another to be our campaign spokesperson. Our ballot argument was signed by seniors. We made an effort to recruit seniors as volunteers to staff the office and to contact voters. Our campaign called every senior citizen in the community and encouraged each one of them to visit the schools. When the votes came in, we received 72% of the vote. Seniors voted to improve the schools, despite the fact that few had children or grandchildren in the schools. We had overcome a stereotype of older voters. By taking a simple message: the need to repair local schools and communicating that message directly to people, we overcame the stereotype that "seniors" would not be supportive.

Our campaign volunteers had proved the insiders and the press wrong. We had succeeded. We spent our time talking to the voters, whether they were young or old, parents or not. The seniors heard directly from us, and they responded with their vote.

Chapter Eighteen

Talk to People, Not the Press

Candidates complain when they do not get press coverage, and when they do get it, they complain when it is not to their liking. Countless hours are devoted to developing a "press strategy," and for the most part, it is a waste of time.

In campaign meetings, where candidates and their supporters complain that an article in the newspaper is unfair (which, by the way, was probably hidden in section B, page 6), I ask the people at the meeting if they read the newspaper every day. Most say they do.

I then ask, "Do you think other people read the newspaper as thoroughly as you read it?" The answer is always "no."

I ask if they read the paper yesterday morning. Most say they did.

I then ask, "What was the top headline on the front page of the newspaper yesterday?" Few can answer. Few remember.

Campaigns obsess about coverage no one reads, and if they did happen to read an article, they usually do not remember what it said. I usually advise my clients that unless they are running for governor or President they should not worry about press coverage—good or bad.

* * * * *

The Poway Unified School District in northern San Diego County is one of California's largest and best school districts. Parents pay premium prices for homes in the district so their children can attend the local schools.

Despite high student achievement and the high quality schools, the school district had been unsuccessful in obtaining voter support for a bond measure, partly because California law requires a super majority YES vote. The district failed twice within a three year period and was cautiously moving forward to place a new measure on the ballot to provide funds to repair aging schools and to provide desperately needed classrooms.

In the spring of 2002, just prior to placing a new measure on the ballot, the Poway School District became the lead story in local newspapers and on San Diego television and radio stations. National media outlets then picked up the story. All major networks—ABC, CBS, NBC, FOX, CNN—carried the story, radio talk show hosts around the country joined the media frenzy, and Jay Leno and Dave Letterman mentioned the school district in their monologues on late night TV.

Dozens of articles were written. *Education Week* carried the story as did the *New York Times*, the *Los Angeles Times* and the *Washington Post*. The wire services UPI and the Associated Press both picked up the story which was covered around the world. The district received hundreds of emails and phone calls. Requests for interviews came in from overseas, and reporters (mostly from outside the district) descended on the district offices every day for two weeks.

What caused this media frenzy? Underwear. That's right, underwear—girls' underwear.

ABC News.com:
"Parents at a California high school are in an uproar amid allegations the female assistant principal lifted the skirts of girls attending a dance to make sure the students were not wearing thong underwear."

Education Week:
"News in brief (no pun intended)
"A California high school administrator was placed on leave last week after she allegedly lifted girls' skirts in front of male students and adults to make sure they were not wearing thong underwear at a school dance."

The superintendent of schools and the Board of Education, to their credit, handled the issue professionally. The administrator was suspended, pending a formal hearing, and thoughtful discussions were encouraged among parents and students as to what constituted proper behavior at school dances and what was the proper role of school administrators.

As for the proposed bond measure, school leaders questioned whether the school district could put a measure on the ballot at this time and have any chance of winning. No one ever had experienced anything quite like this. Media attention was intense and unrelenting. Our campaign leaders were depressed. Some parents were embarrassed, others were angry.

A poll initially scheduled to take place the week of the "incident" was now postponed. One board member said, "I don't want to know what people think of us right now. I know it's bad!" Another member of the Board of Education, at a conference outside the district, was given a gift box that included a thong.

Opponents of the school district attempted to capitalize on the issue, saying the district could not be trusted. Political insiders said the district would be crazy to place a measure on the ballot at this time. The likelihood of taxpayers voting to increase their taxes on behalf of the school district seemed remote.

Nevertheless we kept working as though nothing had happened..

Each school was assessed. Were there enough classrooms? What repairs were needed? Did each school have equitable facilities? The facility committee kept on task and eliminated projects that were not needed or that could be funded from other sources. The district continued to inform citizens about the needs of the schools and the plans for their repair. As the deadline neared to make the decision to put a measure on the ballot, the controversy of the "thong incident" was still in the national press. We had to decide whether or not to place the measure on the ballot. We decided to poll voters on their impression of the district. Many expected the worst.

The results shocked us. Out of 400 voters surveyed only five mentioned the "thong incident." More importantly:

83% said the school district was doing a good or excellent job.

66% understood the need for repairs and renovations.

68% said they would consider supporting a tax increase to renovate the schools.

We decided cautiously to put the measure on the ballot.

The campaign was not easy. Every time there was a negative article in the newspaper about the district, we said, "Remember the thong," reminding our volunteers and staff that despite all the negative press during the thong incident voters still supported the schools. We trusted voters to make distinctions between real issues and the issues the press often focuses on. Our job was to talk to voters and we ignored the press. We were confident we could win if we kept focused and stayed on our message.

In November, just six months after the "thong incident," voters in the Poway Unified School District voted to increase their taxes and approved a $250,000,000 bond to repair and renovate the schools.

* * * * *

During a local race, a candidate we were working with called me and said we needed to respond to a letter that had appeared in the "Letters to the Editor." The letter, she said, clearly misstated her position. I had to admit I had not seen it. Like most people, I glanced at the local news, read the sports section, looked at my horoscope and read the weather report. Damn. I had not read the all-important "Letters to the Editor."

Writing or responding to "Letters to the Editor" usually is a waste of time, but I will never convince anyone of that. The main benefit letters to the editor provide is to improve the morale of campaign workers and the candidate. A well-written letter by someone who supports your candidate or cause can do wonders for volunteers and campaign staff but it does little more.

Few voters change their opinion because of a letter that they read in the newspaper. Letters to the editors serve the same purpose as comics, sports sections and movie reviews—entertainment. Believe it or not, some campaigns actually keep a scorecard of the letters to editors, pro and con, as if at the end of the campaign you could weigh the two stacks and the heaviest wins the election.

* * * * *

Next to having an obsession with press coverage, the second most significant waste of energy are candidate debates and town hall meetings. Except for New Hampshire, Iowa and perhaps a few other places in the country, town hall meetings are of a bygone era. That is not to say that politicians do not conduct town hall meetings. They do. The problem is that most people who attend them either have their minds made up already or have been recruited to come to the meetings by the candidate.

Politicians hold town hall meetings to create an impression that they are staying in touch with their constituents and are "listening." The people who show up are the people who show up all the time. The meetings serve the purpose of providing the elected official with an opportunity to send mail to all voters in the district at the taxpayers expense.

In our Sunday paper, I read about our local congressman who had conducted a town hall meeting. The reporter wrote a long article about the congressman who had announced his opposition to the administration's prescription drug bill at a town hall meeting. Curious, I called the congressman's office and asked how many people attended the town hall meeting. The answer: six.

People do not go to meetings, unless an unwanted freeway is going in, a power plant is spewing toxic fumes, there is a significant increase in crime in the neighborhood, or a casino is being proposed down the road.

Candidates are often asked to go to meetings. While they may serve some purpose, they seldom serve an electoral purpose. Candidates often are merely entertainment for the folks who attend meetings, who rarely listen in between bites of chicken. You cannot build momentum going to meetings. You are also not going to get many new votes. Former California Governor and Oakland Mayor Jerry Brown once told me he went to 39 candidate debates when he first ran for mayor of Oakland, and because of the number of candidates for mayor (9) his allotted time to speak was less than 3 minutes per event.

He saw many of the same people at every candidate night. Some were campaign workers from other campaigns, some had little else to do. A candidate for office will reach more voters by going door-to-door than he or she is likely to meet at a candidate night or a debate.

* * * * *

During one of our campaigns, the "meeting coordinator" for a local Rotary chapter was incensed when I told him that our candidate could not attend his meeting as she was walking precincts that evening, talking to voters.

"But that's impossible," he said. "I don't have another speaker!"

I asked him who had been there last month.

"Oh, last month we had a magician from the high school, he was terrific."

* * * * *

A school district we worked with was convinced that it needed to hold a community meeting to reveal plans for renovating the local schools and to obtain community input. Ten thousand leaflets were sent home with the students to parents informing them of the meeting. Articles announcing the meeting were placed in the paper. When the night came for the meeting only ten people showed up. Four were parents, two were administrators hosting the meeting, and two others were senior citizens who lived across the street from one of the schools. The final two included one opponent of any renovations of the schools, who dominated the meeting, and one reporter who wrote what the opponent had to say in her report of the meeting. The effort put into publicizing the meeting had been wasted. Few people had attended, and the one opponent who attended was able to use the meeting to get press coverage for his viewpoint.

* * * * *

Here are some tips for dealing with the press:
- Do not have a press secretary unless your candidate is running for the Presidency, the U.S. Senate, a governor's office or the mayor of a big city.
- Reporters often say they are "on deadline." This is a tactic to get you to talk to them. Their deadline is not your deadline. Deal with reporters when *you* are ready.
- Anyone who says they know how to deal with the press usually does not.
- Nothing is ever "off the record."
- The farther away the reporter gets from a pad and pencil and closer to a camera, the more superficial the coverage.
- Never allow the spouse of a candidate to speak to the press, especially if it is in response to something negative. (Politics is business, not personal.)
- Be honest; spinning does not work unless you are an ice skater or on an exercise bike.
- If you do not know the answer to a question, tell the reporter you will get back to them.
- Get back to them.
- News articles rarely make or break a campaign. Take them in stride.
- If you feel you have been quoted inaccurately or a story is inaccurate,

call the reporter only when you have chilled out and can speak calmly. Calling the reporter will not do much good, but you might feel better.

- Editorial writers have less influence on voters than they think they have. (Hint: most voters do not read editorials, and those that do usually have their minds made up already).
- Unless a story is in the news for days on end, there is a great chance few people will see it.
- Articles that appear in the newspaper are more closely read by campaign insiders than by actual voters.

* * * * *

Cesar Chavez once described the press to me as a "voracious animal that needs to be fed constantly." Cesar was a master at using the press to further the cause of farm workers. He creatively used the press to make people aware of the plight of farm workers, but he was cautious and never fully trusted the press to accurately report anything but the most superficial stories. He had reporters go to the labor camps to see the wretched conditions. He invited reporters to talk to workers in the fields who were toiling with back breaking work under the hot sun, using short handled hoes. Reporters were always available to record Cesar's fasts and demonstrations. The press was *used* to help define the debate in the public's eye as a battle between rich growers and exploited farm workers. The message never varied.

Cesar knew that political and organizational success was the result of organizing people, not press relations, and so he made each press event an opportunity to organize people or to encourage people to become involved.

Congressman Ron Dellums, Supervisor John George, Cesar Chavez, and California Assembly member Tom Bates going door-to-door raising awareness of the farm workers boycott. Cesar was a master of using the press to draw attention to the plight of farm workers.

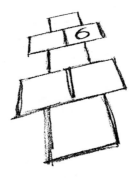

Sidewalk Strategy #6

Invest in People

For the past thirty years, I have been involved in political and community organizing, and I have heard countless theories on how to win elections. In California, the most common advice I hear is: "Every dollar not spent on TV advertising is a wasted dollar." Others say the most important thing to spend money on is polling, while others claim direct mail is critical and the more mail the better.

But in local elections, *people*—campaign staff and willing volunteers— have more influence on winning elections than anything else. Unlike national elections where vast sums of money are spent on television and other media advertising and where candidates rarely connect with people except for "photo ops," local elections are usually won in the trenches through grass roots organizing by committed volunteers. These local elections and the active involvement of citizens are the foundation upon which our democracy is built.

Thirty years ago, it was common to have campaigns run by a friend of the candidate, usually a volunteer who could take a few months off from his or her job. Today, "professional" political advisors are paid to make decisions and to craft the message and theme of the campaign.

Unfortunately, most of the people who are making decisions on political campaigns today have never walked a precinct or talked to a voter on the phone or spent time supervising a phone bank. Few have spent time canvassing neighborhoods or collecting signatures on a petition in front of a supermarket. Experience in direct voter contact is a rare attribute among political consultants and our political process suffers because of it.

Consequently, when campaign budgets and strategies are developed, many consultants have no idea of the power of committed volunteers or the importance of grass roots political action. They choose to spend resources on mail and television but rarely on encouraging participation or voter turnout. (It does not help that consultants receive lucrative commissions from printing and media buys which obviously influence their choice of strategies and decisions on how to allocate campaign dollars.) As campaigns become more obsessed with media coverage and paid advertising, it becomes harder for the average citizen to become involved in the democratic process.

Sidewalk Strategy #6 is about finding and motivating the people who will be the backbone of a successful campaign. Chapter Nineteen provides clues as to how to find and keep good staff, how to develop effective staff and, sadly, how to let someone go when necessary. Recruiting and motivating and keeping good volunteers is the focus of Chapter Twenty. Creating an environment where people want to volunteer takes effort and finding the balance between productive work and an enjoyable experience is a necessity. Chapter Twenty-One is about the blending of grass roots politics with technology and how technology is rapidly changing the way politics, especially grass roots politics, is practiced.

Chapter Nineteen

Finding and Keeping Good Staff

For every celebrated political consultant like James Carville or Karl Rove, there are hundreds of anonymous campaign workers who worked in the campaigns that made them famous. For every Cesar Chavez, there are legions of farm workers and their supporters who volunteered day in and day out building the farm worker movement. For every successful candidate, there are hundreds of people who are never mentioned but who contribute time and energy getting that person elected.

Our political system and many of our greatest public service institutions—hospitals, churches, synagogues, libraries, unions, community recreation and sports programs—are staffed by volunteers or people who work for low pay because they believe in the cause. Finding good volunteers and good staff is not only smart, it is essential for success.

Today's volunteer might become tomorrow's candidate. Today's staff person might become tomorrow's leader. More than a few elected officials started out as interns or volunteers on a campaign.

Developing staff and training volunteers takes work and commitment. Most political consultants do not take this responsibility seriously and prefer to "hire" experienced help who have worked in other political campaigns and seemingly need little direction. Volunteers are rarely involved in staff meetings and are rarely privy to important strategy discussions.

When I was a green organizer with the United Farm Workers, I cherished being in meetings where Cesar Chavez, the legendary Fred Ross, Eliseo Medina, Dolores Huerta, Gilbert Padilla, Jim Drake, Marshall Ganz and others debated and argued strategy. Keeping my mouth shut and my ears open was one of the first things I learned. These people devoted their lives to building a union for farm workers, and I felt privileged to listen in on their discussions. Rarely were they in agreement. Heated arguments often went late into the night. They were, however, united in their desire to win on behalf of the farm workers.

The contribution of volunteers and low paid staff was critical to the success of the fledgling United Farm Workers. Instead of pay, we received an education in organizing, building political power, dealing with adversity and overcoming obstacles. While the pay was non-existent, the hours long and the work difficult, staff and volunteers were valued. The union could not have survived without them.

* * * * *

Finding Good Staff

Developing campaign staff and volunteers who will devote hours to the campaign is essential for success. Finding these people can be a challenge. Experience is good, but enthusiasm and a willingness to work hard are better. Every campaign should strive to include people who have no previous political experience. They often make the best campaign staff despite their inexperience. Conversely, the worst campaign staff are often veterans of past efforts who are either impressed with themselves or who are unwilling to learn anything new.

Potential campaign staff are everywhere if you look for them:
- recent graduates of college looking for something worthwhile to do
- college students who are bored with the academic world and want a challenge
- retired people whose experience and talent will compensate for an inability to work long hours
- leaders in civic activities like the PTA, hospitals and libraries
- The internet has become a clearinghouse for posting job openings and a good place to find potential staff.
- Volunteers and interns who have demonstrated their ability and commitment make excellent staff members.

Quality staff members are rarely found in unemployment lines. If you want good people, you will probably find that they are already working.

Getting these people to take a leave from their jobs or to accept the challenge or excitement of a campaign is a necessity. A 3-6 month commitment on a campaign may indeed change a person's life.

Whatever the responsibility or the experience of individual staff, the important thing is to treat everyone equally. No special treatment for some. No prima donnas. Expectations need to be laid out in the beginning, and those who cannot commit to the effort should not be asked to be staff members. Staff are role models for everyone volunteering on the campaign, and they need to understand this responsibility.

The best employees usually have a combination of job knowledge and good attitude. Those with a good attitude and lesser job knowledge can be worked with and taught. When I started as an organizer, I had no job knowledge, but I had a good attitude. Someone who has good job knowledge but a bad attitude or bad work habits is not worth keeping. In my experience, it is almost impossible to correct a bad attitude, and people with a bad attitude can consume almost all of your time.

One of the applicants for a campaign position for which I was hiring was a graduate of a prestigious university on the East Coast. Barely 22 years old, I asked him what he wanted to be doing in 5 years. "My goal is to be a U.S. senator in 5 years," he informed me matter-of-factly. I wanted to ask him if he knew that 30 was the minimum age to be a U.S. senator, but I decided to pass and instead asked him, "Why do you want to work on this campaign?"

He said it would be important to have on his résumé and that he was hopeful of getting a permanent legislative job at the end of the campaign.

The second applicant was a recent graduate of a state college. He had attended community college and had worked part-time to pay his tuition. I asked him what he wanted to be doing in five years. He said he was not sure, but at this point, he was thinking of teaching. I asked him, "Why do you want to work on this campaign?" His answer: "When I was in college it was difficult to make ends meet. I know a lot of kids who couldn't go to school because they didn't have the money. If we can elect people who care about providing opportunities for people regardless of their economic status, it would really help. I met (the candidate) at school, and he really impressed me with his commitment. I'd like to help."

I hired candidate #2 and never regretted the decision. Inexperienced campaign workers often bring more enthusiasm and energy than those with political ambitions.

Developing Staff

People are always surprised when, at the beginning of a campaign, I put in writing the campaign goal (the number of votes we need to win) and the campaign strategy. Sometimes I am asked, "What if the opposition learns of our strategy?" I always respond that winning is about *implementation* of strategy, not developing it. The key to implementation is making sure everyone working on the campaign, staff and volunteers, has enough knowledge to effectively do what they are asked to do. I am more concerned that our own staff and volunteers know what they are working toward than I am about what our opposition might learn. Sharing strategy with staff encourages their participation and says to them: "You are valuable, thank you for helping."

Daily staff meetings are essential to develop staff. What was accomplished yesterday? What do we want to accomplish today? What important information do we need to share? What did we learn? How can we do our job better? Weekly meetings might be acceptable in a business setting, but they are *never* enough in a campaign. A week is an eternity on a campaign. By the time you find out about something, it is too late to correct a problem or an opportunity is lost.

If training and daily meetings are part of the campaign, inexperienced staff people can be mentored and taught. Daily meetings provide an opportunity for questions to be asked in a timely way and for training to be conducted. Young staff can learn from more experienced staff without hierarchy and ego getting in the way. An inexperienced staff person who has had a success can be acknowledged and praised immediately. The daily meetings provide an opportunity for staff to become successful and to identify problems before they become critical.

Staff meetings are also helpful to determine who really is working and who is not. The people who complain about staff meetings or who are late for them usually turn out to be the problem staff members.

Keeping Staff

Finding staff is just one part of the problem. Keeping them (as most will be working for either low or non-existent pay) and making them effective are larger problems. Here are some of the things I have learned about campaign staff:

If you want good staff, you have to devote effort to train them. Few people have the skills to be effective initially. Most campaign staff do not have vast amounts of experience, so training is absolutely essential.

Allow staff to listen in and participate at "upper level" strategy meetings. Some campaigns operate with a strict hierarchy and allow only those at the top access to information. I believe that the more it is possible to share strategy and goals with staff, the more likely they will be able to implement it.

Do not accept poor quality work or behavior from volunteers. A misconception is that volunteers, because they are not paid, cannot be held accountable. Big mistake. Volunteers, like everyone else in the campaign, must be given specific assignments and objectives, and if those objectives are not reached, those responsible need to be held accountable, even volunteers.

Daily staff meetings are essential. Two key words here—daily and meetings. Political campaigns must make progress on a daily basis. Each day that passes is another day lost. Staff meetings are an essential element of the need to utilize every day effectively. Staff meetings can be used to train staff, discuss strategy, learn from mistakes and successes, and create solidarity and enthusiasm. Staff meetings do not have to be long—an hour or an hour-and-a-half is plenty. An agenda needs to be made and reviewed. Discussions should be crisp.

Require staff to take notes at meetings. Taking notes reduces miscommunications and misinterpretations. In all the years I have been organizing, I have never met anyone with a photographic mind, yet I have seen many staff members attend meetings without taking notes. I have always wondered how they remember things, and usually, they do not.

Treat everybody the same. Although campaign staff may vary in experience and ability, everyone needs to share doing the mundane tasks like taking out the garbage and cleaning out the refrigerator. A good motto is "we all do windows, we all do floors." A campaign is more likely to be torn apart by BIG EGOs and special treatment for some than by attacks from the opposition.

Appreciate the work that campaign staff do. There is very little glamour or financial reward working on a political campaign. The hours are long. The working environment is often less than ideal. Stress is omnipresent. There are egos and conflicts, poor food and limited resources. Yet despite this, campaign staff and volunteers are essential. Make sure they get complimentary passes to the big events, and make sure the candidate takes time to speak with them.

Treat them like the stars you want them to be.

Letting Staff Go

To keep good staff, sometimes you have to let the bad ones go. As my mentor, Fred Ross Sr., used to say, "If you have a staff person who takes more energy than they give, you have got to let them go."

Fred would say that the process is like cultivating plants in a garden. You want to nurture the hardy plants to create a great garden; treat the others like weeds and pull them out so they do not sap the strength of the other plants. By taking out the weeds, you give the hardy ones even more strength to grow.

Firing someone is one of the hardest things to do in a campaign. Unfortunately, it sometimes has to happen. Campaigns are not the place for people to be working out personal problems, and they definitely are not the place for people who are not contributing to the win.

If you think "firing" a paid campaign staff member is hard, try firing an unpaid volunteer. Some people are just not cut out to talk to voters, and others want to do a good job but are too busy doing other things to fulfill their commitment.

* * * * *

We had been hired to run a campaign on behalf of a hospital district. One of the internists, a young female doctor, volunteered to talk to her neighbors. She was assigned her own precinct and was instructed to keep detailed notes of who was supportive and who opposed. Days passed, and we received no reports from her, despite numerous calls. Finally, we reached her, and she said, understandably, she had been busy and would get to it over the weekend. On Monday we called again. An emergency had happened at the hospital, and she still had not done the work. Election Day was nearing, and the vote was going to be close. Her precinct was a swing precinct for us, and we had to have someone work it.

Telling her she had to relinquish her precinct was not going to be easy. She was a doctor, she was employed by the hospital, she wanted to save the hospital, and she had the best intentions. The simple truth was that she was not doing the work, and despite everything else, her lack of effort was hurting our chances.

As is often the case, being honest and direct was the best approach. We told her that we understood she was busy, but we had to have someone we could depend on. If she wanted to volunteer when she had time that was great, but for now, we were turning her precinct over to someone else. I think she was relieved.

Just because someone is "volunteering" does not mean the acceptance of poor quality work or behavior. By tolerating poor work from a volunteer, you send a message to other volunteers that either the work you are asking them to do is not important or that poor quality effort is acceptable. The higher the standard you demand, the higher the quality of effort and work you will get.

Not All Help is Useful

Every campaign has a unique blend of personalities, and there are some that will almost always derail the campaign if you let them. They include:

- The Legal Beavers: "Have we checked whether it is permissible to go door-to-door?"
- The Queen Mothers: "I want to be in charge of everything, but I can only help from 5 to 6 on Tuesdays and Thursdays."
- The Aspiring Candidates: "I'd be glad to let you use my name, but I'm really too busy to help."
- The Business Leaders: "If only this campaign were run the way I run MY business …"
- The Ms. and Mr. Pessimists: "Nothing is going right."
- The Social Butterfly: "I'll be happy to attend the fundraiser (for free) but I just *can't* call voters."

Every campaign attracts "experts," and each of them has ideas and opinions of what it will take to win:

- "We absolutely need bumper stickers."
- "I can predict who will win by which campaign puts up the most signs."
- "There are going to be 50,000 people at the big game. We *must* have a banner pulled by an airplane saying vote YES."
- "We must attend *every* candidate debate. If we don't, we will lose!"
- "Next week is Founders Day celebration in the park. We absolutely need balloons."

It would be nice if campaigns attracted the best and the brightest, but sometimes they do not. Campaigns often attract people for the wrong reasons. Some are attracted because they want to be close to the candidate who may be a celebrity. Some are trawling for their own contacts to feed their own personal career ambitions. Campaigns attract sycophants and hangers on, wannabes and self-important know-it-alls, ideologues and egomaniacs. Some people are just damn lazy and want to hang around a headquarters and get in the way. Political campaigns are not the place to receive or give therapy or counseling. The goal is to win, and the individual needs of staff and volunteers must take a back seat.

Four cardinal sins you cannot allow on your campaign
Lying * Stealing * Abusing People * Not working hard

Lies can tear a campaign apart. Aside from the political ramifications of having a staff member lie, the campaign demands honest evaluations of what is going on. Anyone who lies about reports or any other matter should be dismissed from the campaign as soon as possible.
Lies are usually in the form of exaggeration. "I made 50 calls and everybody was supportive." Letting your staff know that honesty (even bad news: "I made 8 calls and 7 were opposed.") is more important than inaccurate optimistic reports.

Theft cannot be tolerated. Campaigns, by their nature, need to be open. Volunteers and staff work long hours, often in less than ideal working conditions. Anyone stealing anything from a volunteer or the campaign needs to be ushered out immediately.
A campaign where volunteers have to keep an eye on their purses will soon not have any volunteers. Theft of polls, campaign data and confidential materials can never be tolerated.

Treating people with respect, whether they are volunteers or staff, is essential in campaigns. In all the years Fred Ross grilled me about my performance, he rarely yelled. His piercing eyes and probing questions told me he respected my work and wanted my best effort. Fred expected people to be on time and ready to work. If we were not, he made sure we knew we were not respecting the other people who had arrived on time and were ready to work.

Campaigns can be stressful, and some loss of temper and frayed nerves is excusable. Nevertheless, anyone who has a pattern of anger should not be part of a campaign. Campaigns should not be "touchy feely" either. Part of treating people with respect is demanding their best effort and their best work.

Nothing is more disruptive to a campaign than a staff person who does not work hard. There are countless excuses people make for their lack of effort, and none can be tolerated. A staff person sets the example for volunteers.

Campaigns are hard work. The difference between winning and losing is often due to the extra effort that people make. A staff person who complains constantly will eventually infect the whole campaign. It is usually necessary to replace such a person.

Set the Example

Organizers who do not lead by example are like generals asking soldiers to go to the front when they have never been in battle themselves. Whether it is walking precincts, talking to voters or asking people to work on Election Day, an effective leader volunteers first, takes the toughest assignments and sets the example for others.

A campaign organizer or candidate who leads by example encourages others to participate. I encourage our candidate clients to come to our phone banks to call voters side-by-side with the volunteers or to walk door-to-door with volunteers. I encourage superintendents of school districts that have placed tax measures on the ballot to volunteer along with the parents and teachers. No one is too important to talk to voters, and if you want volunteers in your campaign, you not only have to ask them, you have to be willing to set the example.

Chapter Twenty

Value Volunteers

Managing resources successfully is as important in a political campaign as it is in business. Time, money and people are the three most important resources a candidate or a campaign has to work with, and of the three, the most underutilized is people. Campaigns spend enormous effort and time raising money to spend on mail and media, and precious little effort and time recruiting quality people to volunteer on behalf of the campaign. This is true despite the fact that *local* elections are usually won or lost not by the campaign that spends the most money, but rather, the campaign that is able to motivate and manage large numbers of volunteers. Effective work by volunteers is often the difference between winning and losing. Recruiting, training and motivating volunteers are crucial skills that must be developed.

I often think of my father as the prototypical "undecided" voter. Neither political mail nor television spots could persuade him to vote one way or another. Political mail usually ended up in the garbage can, and he would regularly hang-up on telemarketers. Like most voters, he did not attend community meetings, candidate debates or belong to political clubs. He was not persuaded by editorial endorsements or what "slate cards" recommended. What had an impact on him, though, was a visit from a respected neighbor, someone intelligent and articulate, who could answer his questions and win his trust and his vote. Sometimes it took more than one visit. He respected someone taking the time to talk with him and answer his questions.

Over the years, I have learned that, in this respect, my father was not unique. He responded the way most people do to personal contact, and while it is in vogue for campaigns to utilize pre-recorded automated phone calls to voters and to hire "paid precinct walkers," real volunteers, who are committed to the campaign and know the community, are far more effective.

A motivated volunteer who has been adequately trained is often able to convince a "no" voter to vote "yes." An articulate volunteer can provide undecided voters with information to persuade them to vote for a candidate or an issue. Unfortunately, many campaigns invest very little time and effort in recruiting, training and managing volunteers, despite election results that prove the difference in winning and losing elections is often a few votes or at most a few percentage points.

Many of the elections my company has won would have been lost had we not had the help of dedicated volunteers who were able to persuade "undecided" voters to become "yes" votes or who were successful in getting people out to vote who would not otherwise have voted.

If volunteers are so critical to success why don't campaign consultants make a bigger effort to involve people or recruit volunteers? There are four primary reasons:

They do not know how.

It takes too much effort.

It is not glamorous.

There is no money in it.

Today, political campaigns are managed by specialists. There are media experts, opposition research specialists, direct mail consultants, image consultants, fund raisers, public opinion researchers, public relations experts and telemarketing specialists. Multi-million dollar industries have been developed to provide election campaigns with assistance in everything from automated calls to handwritten letters, yet it is rare to find a campaign where there is a specialist to recruit and organize people.

Finding volunteers is not difficult, if the effort and commitment is made to do so.

Finding Volunteers

I recently ran into a person at a coffee shop who had volunteered on a political campaign that I had worked on years earlier. As we sipped our coffee, he told me he was now working for the Department of Social Services helping families get back on their feet. He told me that the campaign he had worked on changed his life. Prior to the campaign, he knew little about the electoral process, but through his work as a volunteer, he learned how to involve people and how to bring about change. He told me he now tries to use these lessons each day at work.

I asked him how it was that he first became a volunteer. He told me, "Someone asked me. It was that simple." He had registered to vote in a presidential election, and the person who had registered him asked if he was interested in volunteering. He never thought of it before. He told them that he had some free time, and later that week, he received a call asking him to help register other voters. A simple question and a follow-up call got him involved politically.

* * * * *

Some years after I left the UFW, I was working on a campaign for Dianne Feinstein. At that time, she was mayor of San Francisco (she is now a U.S. senator), and she was facing a "re-call election" forced by a political fringe group. About three weeks before the election, we needed additional volunteers to help get-out-the-vote. It was clear that if we were going to get more volunteers we had to be more aggressive about asking people to help. Fred Ross, Sr., who was in his seventies at the time, was providing guidance and training to the campaign staff. Under Fred's tutelage, we had our staff call voters during the day. They were instructed to say, "Mrs. [Jones], I'm calling you on behalf of Mayor Feinstein. We have an emergency, and Mayor Feinstein's campaign needs your help. The election is just a few weeks away, and we are worried the Mayor will lose. Your precinct is one of the most important in the city, and we need you to help us on Election Day, right in your neighborhood, reminding people to vote. You'll help us, won't you?" We figured anybody we found at home probably was not working during the day and would therefore be available to help us.

Although we blindly called voters (the lists we were using were simply those of registered voters), perhaps one person out of five we reached said "yes." If they were interested, we immediately went to their house and explained face-to-face what we wanted them to do. We recruited over 100 precinct leaders this way and hundreds of Election Day volunteers, few of whom had ever volunteered on a campaign before. Ultimately, through the

Fred Ross Sr. came out of retirement to help train staff and volunteers when San Francisco Mayor Diane Feinstein was forced into a recall campaign. This was one of the last major organizing efforts Ross worked on before his death in 1992.

At one of our Saturday mobilizations on behalf of Mayor Feinstein, I introduced a farm worker representative from Salinas who presented Mayor Feinstein with a donation.

efforts of these volunteers and others, we were able to turn out a record number of voters for a special election, and Mayor Feinstein won in a landslide.

As part of the training to recruit volunteers, Fred made us all go visit the homes of people who had agreed to volunteer—myself included. As Fred told me, "If you don't go, your staff will not take the work seriously. They won't believe it can be done. You've got to model behavior. Never ask people to do something you're unwilling to do yourself."

* * * * *

During the mayoral campaign for Elihu Harris in Oakland, California, our candidate learned a painful lesson of how *not* to treat volunteers.

I was managing the voter contact effort for the campaign, and our plan was to build a volunteer army that would help elect Elihu mayor. Each Saturday, we asked volunteers to attend a meeting to talk about the campaign, hear reports of what we were doing, and then, they were dispatched out to walk precincts or call voters. Elihu was a member of the California State Assembly at the time, and although he never walked precincts himself, he did speak to the volunteers at our meetings.

Volunteers were asked to come at 10:00 A.M. to meet the other volunteers and have a cup of coffee, juice and pastry. The meetings started at 10:30 A.M. sharp. We introduced people and explained what we wanted to accomplish that day. Elihu would normally show up at about 11:00, (he did not want to sit through the reports or introductions of volunteers). While it was awkward, we unfortunately allowed it to happen.

One Saturday, about a month before the election, we called a special meeting to inspire people and kickoff the last push to the election. About 250 volunteers showed up. As usual, the volunteers arrived about 10-10:15 for the 10:30 meeting. By eleven, we had completed our reports, gone over the details of the day, and by 11:20, our candidate still had not arrived. By 11:30, I knew we had a problem. We had introduced everyone, once again explained what we were doing that day—and still no Elihu. As the volunteers were getting antsy (they in fact had other things they wanted to do on their day off work once our work was completed), I dispatched the people to the phone banks and to walk precincts, telling them our candidate had been delayed at another important meeting.

While most of the volunteers understood, there was some grumbling.

One person said he had taken time off work because he wanted to ask Elihu a question that someone had asked him and that he could not answer. Another volunteer had brought her son and wanted to introduce him to the next mayor. One of our best volunteers came up to me after the meeting and said, "If Elihu doesn't think we are important enough to come on a Saturday, then I don't want to volunteer anymore!"

Our volunteers were there because they wanted to help, not because they had nothing better to do. Among them were teachers, city workers, truck drivers and day-care providers who were volunteering on their day off for a campaign they thought was important.

At five minutes to noon our candidate and his wife, Kathy Neal, strolled into the headquarters carrying Nordstrom bags. Only a few volunteers were left in the office, as everyone else had been dispatched out. I asked Elihu where he had been. "Shopping," was his sheepish reply.

Mrs. Neal was incensed we had allowed people to leave. "Where is everybody?" she asked. "You dispatched the volunteers? Before WE arrived?"

"But Kathy," I replied, "some people have been here for two hours and they, too, have things that they need to do. If we didn't dispatch them to the precincts, they would have gone home."

I told Elihu that if we were going to have a successful campaign, he had to make it a priority to come on Saturdays, on time from now on and to be there for the volunteers. To his credit, he learned from that experience, and went on to win the election and to serve two terms as mayor of Oakland. Even after the election, he made an effort to keep his volunteers involved, conducting regular meetings and briefings with them.

* * * * *

In San Francisco every Election Day, Allegro restaurant hosts a "Political Hacks" luncheon. Political consultants, candidates, elected officials, financial contributors, reporters and insiders on all sides of issues and campaigns come together to tell stories, posture among themselves and place bets on who will win. I never attend, even though the owner of Allegro's is a friend of mine.

Why? The luncheon is on Election Day! On Election Day, there are voters to be reminded to vote, rides to give to the elderly, phone calls to make and doors to knock on. Work should end at 8 P.M. when the polls close, not a minute before. Countless elections are won or lost in the last hours of Election

Day. Can you imagine asking volunteers to work all day on Election Day and then you take off to have lunch with your opposition?

If volunteers are lucky, they may get a slice of pizza and a coke on Election Day. Meanwhile, the political insiders are dining on fettuccini with clam sauce. It happens all the time. It happens because too many consultants and candidates do not respect the work of volunteers, do not feel obligated themselves to do what they are asking others to do and worse still, value financial contributors more than volunteers.

Respect the Work of Volunteers.
Candidates often have more respect for their financial contributors than for the people who volunteer time on their campaign. Financial donors are treated to special events, intimate get-togethers and catered dinners, while campaign volunteers, who spend hours on the phone or going door-to-door, are lucky to get a thank you or a donut for their efforts. Something is out of whack when those who have money get more attention than those who give something so precious they will never get back—their time.

During one mayoral campaign that attracted national attention, on Election night about two hours *before* the polls closed, people (most of whom I had never seen before) began arriving at our headquarters dressed in their party finest. Among them were people who never volunteered or worked on the campaign. It was clear our candidate was going to win, and these people were coming expecting a party. Polls would be closed at 8 P.M. We had two hours left to work.

Since our volunteers were still working feverishly in the neighborhoods getting people out to vote, I ordered the party-goers out of the headquarters and locked the doors. We politely told people that we would open the headquarters and begin partying at 8 P.M. when the polls closed and not a minute sooner.

At 8:15 streams of volunteers, tired and hungry, came back to the headquarters to give their reports. They were escorted to the front of the hall where we had reserved places of honor for them. The party-goers could wait at the back. Our volunteers who had worked all day deserved to be treated with respect.

* * * * *

Ask an administrator at a hospital if the hospital could run without volunteers, and he would say no. Most athletic and recreation programs for children are run by volunteers. Volunteers in classrooms provide additional adult supervision and more individual attention to students. Volunteers keep charities alive and food banks functioning. Without volunteers local political campaigns would be hard pressed to contact voters. Volunteers give money and time, and for their efforts, they receive very little attention and respect. Giving volunteers the respect they deserve is rule one for anyone running for office or anyone running a campaign.

Volunteers are often the difference between winning and losing, so it is essential to know how to use them. Here are some tips on recruiting and developing volunteers:

Make sure volunteers have meaningful work. Nothing will discourage volunteers more than being asked to do something that is not important. When they finish their work, take the time to have them give a report on what they accomplished. If the work is important enough to ask them to do, it is important enough to listen to what they accomplished. If you ask people to come at a specific time, be prepared to put them to work. People's time should not be wasted. Meetings should start on time.

Provide instruction and supervision. Know what you want people to accomplish and why. If the work is important enough to do, it is important enough to let people know why they are doing it. People need to know how what they are doing fits into the bigger picture. It is hard to be productive if you feel your work is not important. Volunteers should be given training on how to do their job, particularly if it involves talking to voters. Few people are effective ad-libbing. An effective organizer trains volunteers on how to speak to voters and provides a volunteer with a script and with answers to tough questions. Good supervision is a necessity.

Be available when volunteers come in. Stick around to greet the last volunteer and to make that last volunteer feel important. Take the time to listen to what volunteers accomplished. Always get reports. Find out what was accomplished and what they learned. Getting reports says to volunteers that their work is valued and respected. It allows the campaign to monitor progress and identify potential problems. Reporting completes the circle of information and validates the importance of the work.

Listen to people. People appreciate the opportunity to be heard. It means their opinion counts. It means they matter. Volunteers can provide important intelligence about what is happening at the grass roots level.

Make sure each volunteer that helps is recognized and thanked individually. People have names, use them. Do not thank "all the volunteers who came." Thank "Bob and Juan, Julia and Bill." Thank people individually for volunteering. Make sure they know their help is appreciated and needed. Look for things to praise. Make sure people know that their effort is appreciated and valued.

Feed people. For a little cost and a little effort, provide food. It will encourage people to stay longer, and they are likely to return. Good food, not junk food, is essential. Armies need more than donuts or pizzas and so do volunteers. Celebrate the day's successes over a meal. Every occasion where volunteers are asked to contribute time, they should be offered something to eat. Providing food is respectful, it is polite, and it is smart. A person who volunteers once is valuable. A person who volunteers twice is twice as valuable. Feed them, they will come back. (Note: Keep alcohol away from the campaign headquarters. Having a good time is one thing, but alcohol and campaigns do not mix. Alcohol impairs judgment, and impaired judgment leads to mistakes.)

Do not ever ask people to do something you are unable or unwilling to do yourself. Too often "leaders" assign tasks to people but are afraid to do the work themselves. Precinct walking or talking to people on the street or on the phone is tough work. A leader knows how to do it and is willing to do it as well. Volunteers are not free labor. If you are unwilling to do something (phone voters, walk precincts, collect petitions on a street corner) chances are volunteers will not be willing to either.

If you want people to volunteer, you have to ask them. When volunteers help, make sure to sign them up again with specific dates and times. The only thing more valuable than a volunteer is a volunteer who volunteers more than once. The more often people volunteer, the better they become.

Invest effort into making sure people who volunteer are successful. If they are, they will be more likely to volunteer again.

Recruit people at all events and activities. Never pass up an opportunity to ask people to volunteer. On the phone, door-to-door, at meetings, collecting signatures, these are all good opportunities to ask people to volunteer.

Use house meetings to recruit staff and volunteers. House meetings are the best way to recruit people into a campaign, if done correctly. House meetings are small get-togethers of 10-20 people in the home of the host. The host should specifically invite people he or she feels could become active in the campaign. The primary purpose of these meetings is to recruit people and to build the campaign. The candidate, or in an issue campaign, the campaign organizer, speaks about the campaign, answers questions and then asks every person at the meeting to volunteer in the campaign. Not all will volunteer, but some will. Most people are surprised to be asked, some are embarrassed. But if you do not ask, few people will volunteer on their own. Who knows? The person who has been recruited to help might turn out to be your best volunteer. It may even change their life. It happens all the time.

Look for opportunities to create fun and excitement. If you create an environment where people want to be, chances are people will return. There is no reason volunteering should not be fun.

Creating a campaign environment where people want to participate takes effort. It does not happen spontaneously, and it does not happen if the campaign leadership (or the candidate) does not believe it is important. Campaigns are not purely about issues, position papers, press releases, campaign brochures and advertising. They are also about reaching out to and involving people in the political process.

Know what you want to use volunteers for when you start the campaign. If you anticipate your election to be close, it is be a good idea to develop a well-trained volunteer base that will be large enough to get people out to vote. If your campaign attempts to persuade voters one way or another, your volunteers will need to be trained how to persuade. It will be essential to develop answers to commonly asked questions. You also need to supervise your volunteers to ensure that only those who are qualified answer voters' questions.

Our entire democratic system requires that citizens become involved politically. Voting is just one aspect of civic participation, volunteering is yet another. But it is a rare individual who volunteers on her own without first being asked. Use every opportunity to ask people to help. Ask for volunteers at every activity and in every mailing. At every meeting, an appeal should be made asking for volunteers. Phone calls to voters should end with the question: "Would you be willing to volunteer a couple hours to help us?" or as Fred Ross would say: "You'd be willing to help, wouldn't you?

* * * * *

People snicker when I tell them that one of the most important assignments on a political campaign should be the "fun coordinator." FUN coordinator? My nickname, at times, has been "Ayatollah Tramutola," a name derived from my disciplined approach to winning. They must think I have gone off my rocker or have gotten soft.

The average person would never consider working on a political campaign. One respected colleague once told me that the only people who volunteer on a campaign are people looking for a job, people who have a personal financial interest in the outcome or people who have no life.

THAT IS NOT TRUE! Democracy is built on the premise that the "common person" must participate in the political process. Many campaigns today are so media and mail driven that there is no place for the "common person" to participate. Many people complain that political campaigns in America have become stale, if not outright boring. That does not have to be the case. Campaigns should be fun. Win or lose, people should look back on their effort and say, "I had a good time. It was worthwhile. I'm glad I did it." Participating in our democracy should be something that brings out the best in people. There is no reason it should not be fun.

I recently ran into a person at our local grocery store who came up to me and said, "I was a volunteer on a campaign you ran 10 years ago. It was the most fun I ever had. It was a great experience."

I asked him why.

He said he felt he had contributed something worthwhile, but more importantly, he had fun. "There was music and food. People worked hard, but they laughed and wanted to come back." He said that he felt a sense of community, and when the campaign was over, he missed the camaraderie, the excitement and the sense of purpose.

In every campaign there are countless opportunities for fun. The fun coordinator understands the campaign objectives and strives to create an atmosphere where good work is done and a good time is had. The fun coordinator's work contributes to the campaign goals and does not distract people from their work. They know the difference between productive fun and fun for fun's sake.

Here are the things that the fun coordinator should do:

Each person who volunteers should be thanked *at the time* for volunteering. Most people have a lot of other things to do and are making a decision to work a few hours on a campaign. Someone needs to be in charge of making them feel special. Treat people well, and they will come back.

Make sure that at every event where there are people, and where it is practical to do so, each person is introduced—by name. Acknowledge and recognize the efforts that people have made. Recognize the oldest volunteer, the youngest, the person who has volunteered the most times. Did anybody volunteer on his or her birthday? If so, make them feel special.

Before events and afterwards make sure there is music.

At every volunteer get-together have a drawing where one or several people can win something. It does not have to be expensive: a campaign poster autographed by the candidate, a dozen donuts. During one campaign where we swept the streets, we gave away brooms. At another where we used ironing boards as portable tables to collect signatures, we presented our top signature gatherer a "gold plated" (painted!) ironing board. Prepare "thank you" bags full of treats for volunteers. Make someone "Queen or King of the Day" and have her wear a crown.

Make the headquarters festive. Have balloons, and give them away. All the volunteers should have their names posted on the volunteer wall of fame. In one school tax measure campaign, someone drew an enormous tree on a wall, and all the volunteers had their names put on a cut out of an apple which was placed on the tree ceremoniously. The tree became the focal point of the headquarters, and apples eventually completely covered the tree.

Photograph courtesy of Dennis Hearne Photography

Incumbent mayor Dianne Feinstein beat a recall attempt by organizing hundreds of volunteers to work on her behalf. Here, Fred Ross Jr. and I instruct volunteers how to collect "vote-by-mail" applications. The thermometer behind me displayed a running total of our progress, and the charts on the walls acknowledged the names of all our volunteers.

Have someone make a video of all your activity. Give away T-shirts, buttons or caps. (My daughters fight over a 30-year-old T-shirt that my wife got on a "March for Justice.")

At every opportunity, discuss what you are trying to do, and measure your progress toward your goal. If you are trying to talk to 10,000 voters on the phone, celebrate at various milestones: 1,000, 2,500, 5,000 etc.

Hilda Sugarman, a Board of Education member from the Fullerton Elementary School District served as the "Fun Coordinator" for our Measure CC campaign. Every night she sent an email to volunteers providing humerous, inspiring and important updates. Her communications were critical to the success of our campaign. Highlights of some of her "communiqués are included in the Appendix on page 228.

Before going out to precinct walk or before making telephone calls, do role-playing. Make it funny and fun. Have someone play the role of the "NO" voter.

During one campaign where one of the candidates refused to debate, his opponent had someone go to every public event the candidate attended dressed in a chicken suit with the opponents' name on the front. After the events, the chicken came back to the headquarters and "crowed" about what happened. It was a riot.

Encourage children and students to participate. Find activities that are appropriate for their age. Children can make signs, cut out paper apples and tie balloons. Older kids can be particularly effective if they are properly trained and supervised. In one bond measure campaign, a high school biology class took responsibility for several precincts and went door-to-door talking to voters about the poor condition of their school's science classrooms.

* * * * *

The Importance of Food

Any time volunteers are asked to come to meetings there should be refreshments. If your budget is tight, get people to volunteer to provide food. I am not talking about Krispy Kremes either. I am talking about real food. In all the years I worked for the UFW, we never paid for food, although we ate well. Somebody was assigned the responsibility of "organizing" food. Many people who would never walk a precinct, volunteered to prepare food for the campaign workers. The food, hot and healthy, nourished many volunteers. After a full day of working, our meals became a communal celebration of hope and thanks.

Food can be a powerful organizing tool. During my early organizing days, I was assigned to San Jose to build support for the farm workers. Each week, the Union would send 50 to 100 farm workers and their families to leaflet stores and picket asking people not to buy non-union lettuce. Not only did we have to provide logistics of dispatching and managing these workers, we had to find housing (free) and food (free) for all who came.

I quickly learned that a peanut butter sandwich and an apple were not sufficient for the workers. We organized a group of women who would take responsibility for preparing the meals. A network of sympathetic restaurants and stores was established that would provide us with either cooked food or the ingredients to prepare it ourselves. While we were out picketing or leafleting, a small army of people worked feverishly to prepare hot food for our return.

During all the years I worked in the UFW, food was an important part of our organizing. At every rally or gathering made up of any significant number of people, there was a feast of inexpensive but nourishing food—beans and rice, tortillas, potatoes, eggs and chicken. These communal feasts were born out of necessity. Many of the workers were poor, and the meals provided sustenance for all. Miraculously, we fed all who came—workers, supporters, union staff and volunteers. The meals were a time for reflection of what we had accomplished that day. Stories were told of people who had helped us and of those who opposed our efforts.

As I began organizing political campaigns, food became an important part of building a grass roots army. Getting someone to volunteer *once* in a campaign is good, but getting people to come back time and again is harder. Providing food for people increases the chances that a volunteer will return. It is not just courteous, it is smart organizing. People will stay longer, enjoy it more and return more frequently if they are treated with respect.

In one mayor's race we ran, we had a different food theme each Saturday—Chinese one week, Italian the next, then Thai, Soul, etc. After the Saturday workday, volunteers were treated to a feast that had been brought into the headquarters. It cost us nothing, only the time to ask restaurants or supporters to prepare it. I learned years earlier that you can get almost anything if you ask, and food is something that people liked to provide. We made a big deal out of acknowledging those who had donated.

Food was served buffet style, and we made sure the candidate helped serve the food. "Thanks for coming," he said as people went through the line. For many of our volunteers, the experience of being served by their future mayor was a memory that lasted a lifetime.

Fred Ross taught me an organizing tool years ago to guarantee a good turnout for a meeting or for a volunteer activity. When reminding people to come ("reminding is the essence of organizing" he made me repeat again and again), ask them to bring something.

"Mary, could you bring a pot of beans for 15?"

"Robert, could you bring a stack of tortillas?

"Vivian, we're counting on you to bring a salad for 10."

"Could you bring something for dessert Bill? We'll need enough for 20."

Today, we have become more organized and sophisticated. We get restaurants to help, special committees are organized to make sure there is enough food and that people are treated with respect and appreciation. The principle is the same. If you are asking people to volunteer, you must feed them. Whatever effort you put into treating people well will be more than returned in their extra effort and commitment to the cause.

You can get a person to volunteer *once* if you are persistent and your cause is a good one. Getting the same person to volunteer a second time or a third or a fourth takes real effort. Creating an environment where people want to volunteer rarely happens spontaneously.

Chapter Twenty-One

Volunteers and Technology

In 2003, the national media became aware of a grass roots phenomenon that has been dramatically increasing in influence: the impact of the Internet on politics.

In February and March of 2003, millions of Americans took part in marches, demonstrations, petitioning, letter writing and protests in an attempt to stop America's impending war on Iraq. The organizers of the protests were not charismatic leaders who motivated the masses with fiery speeches or savvy veteran political organizers but thousands of ordinary Americans, many of whom had never participated in politics. Through cyberspace and the power of the Internet, a grass roots movement involving thousands of people sprung up almost instantaneously and influenced the national debate.

The Internet, and the ability it provides people to communicate directly with others, is rapidly changing the face of politics and political debate.

- In February of 2003, $400,000 was raised in less than 48 hours, at an average of $36 per donor, to place an ad in the New York Times urging more time for UN inspections in Iraq.
- A year earlier, $4.1 million was raised by the organization MoveOn.org to support progressive candidates for congress around the country. To date, MoveOn.org has over 750,000 members, and it expects that donations to candidates will increase to $10 million in the 2004 elections.
- In the spring of 2003, 700,000 people signed on-line petitions in a matter of days voicing opposition to the war in Iraq.

- Millions of Americans, on a daily basis, downloaded information about the war. The Internet allowed people access to information and instant two-way communication, and they used it to organize grass roots efforts across the country.

As more households gain access, the ability of the Internet to coordinate and promote local grass roots activism has only just begun to be tapped.

At a public transit station, an older woman handed me a leaflet urging me to come to a peace vigil. I noticed the leaflet was similar, although slightly different from one that had been left on the doorstep of my home earlier in the week urging me to attend a different protest at a different place and time. I asked the woman if she represented an organization. "Oh no," she replied, "I'm doing this because I don't want to see this country go to war." I told her I had received a similar leaflet at my home, but it was for a different vigil. "There are hundreds of vigils and protests going on," she said. " I printed this one up after seeing one on the Internet."

I asked her if she had ever been involved in a political protest before. "Oh God, no. This is the first time. I got involved after receiving an email from my daughter, and I started communicating with other people on the Internet. There are thousands of us who feel the same way."

It is not just the protesters who used the Internet. Supporters of President Bush and the war in Iraq organized their own web sites and urged Americans to support the war and the policies of the Bush administration. The power of the Internet and technology is changing American politics and providing people not only with more information but also the ability to participate in politics.

Since the founding of this country, political debate has adapted as technology has changed. In the early days of our country, debate was likely to take place at the general store or the town square. Later, radio and television emerged as effective and efficient means to communicate. The power to reach millions of people with simple messages was not lost on political leaders and politicians who spent millions of dollars on TV and radio advertising.

In the new millennium, people are more likely to debate issues and to get involved through the Internet.

When I began organizing years ago, my technology was a notebook and a pencil. Leaflets took hours to create and were reproduced by hand on smelly, smudgy "ditto" or mimeograph machines. A technological advance occurred when we went from dialing on rotary phones to touch-tone phones. The technology an individual has at his fingertips today rivals anything any political party has ever had. Research, information on candidates and issues, ability to communicate with thousands of people at a low cost, ability to raise money, organize letter writing or protests are all possible without much more than a computer and access to the Internet.

Today, the Internet allows people to research issues quickly and efficiently on their own, to talk to others who share beliefs and who may want to become involved, and to participate directly in debate with others thousands of miles away or in the same neighborhood. It is emerging as the most important political tool of our time. Where once it took an organizer weeks to organize a rally, today it can be achieved in just a matter of hours.

Most political campaigns these days have a web site to provide information to voters, and increasingly, voters are choosing to do their own research on candidates and issues by searching the Internet rather than relying solely on information provided by candidates or campaigns.

City council and planning commission meeting notes are routinely posted on the Internet allowing citizens to review important decisions. Parents are able to independently research the qualifications of a new superintendent or principal or to measure the progress of the repairs promised at a local school. Public officials are able to provide constituents with information on issues of concern and to get important feed back from them.

While there is tremendous power in the Internet, there are important limitations to its use politically. Many people are not connected to the Internet, and others who are do not use it. Political action spawned by the Internet has generally been a white upper middle class phenomenon and has yet to reach all segments of our society. The Internet has become yet another source of information for the very knowledgeable and involved few. In some ways, this has further widened the gap between the active and the disenfranchised. While "Internet organizing" can speed communication and reach people almost effortlessly, it does not substitute for old-fashioned person-to-person organizing. It is almost *too* easy to communicate with people. Mobilizing people to go to a march or sign an on-line petition is one thing, registering people to vote then getting them out to vote is another. One takes little effort, the other takes a lot.

The real power of the Internet is the ability to merge instant, low-cost communication with direct face-to-face political action: the blending of technology with old-fashioned political organizing. Voter data, easily available online from local county election departments can be sorted to exclude people who do not vote or who always vote so that campaigns can focus limited resources on the people they need to win.

Whether it is Internet organizing or the old fashioned approach, the basics are still the same: organize around a cause people can believe in, keep the message simple and clear, provide people something meaningful to do and ask others to get involved. The woman who stopped to talk to me at the transit station, encouraged through the Internet to become involved politically and to talk to citizens face-to-face, was an example of a new step in democratic participation. We are likely to see more and more examples in the future.

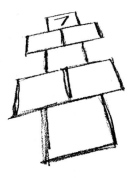

SIDEWALK STRATEGY #7

WIN OR LOSE, KEEP WORKING

One of the most important lessons I learned is that both winning and losing are temporary situations, and the good organizer learns from both successes and from failures. Winning provides an opportunity to do the things you promised or hoped to accomplish: building better schools, involving people into the political process or improving city services. Losing also provides important opportunities and lessons *if* the time is taken to evaluate the loss.

Chapter Twenty-Two is about how to learn from losing and not being afraid or unwilling to accept a defeat and absorb the lessons the defeat provides. Losses often provide the best learning opportunities. Most successful candidates have experienced losing at some time or another in their careers.

Few public agencies (school districts, college districts and local governmental agencies) do an adequate job communicating to voters unless they need something from them. Most elected officials are just as bad. When voters say, "They don't keep their promises once they get elected," it means the elected officials have not kept communicating after an election. Chapter Twenty-Three is about keeping those promises.

The final chapter of the book is a challenge: make a difference by getting involved yourself and not waiting for others. Political success is not about making a name for yourself or becoming famous; it is about working to improve your community. Our democratic society is based on the belief that citizens must participate in civic affairs. Each generation has an obligation to provide for the next and to instill in the new generation a desire to participate. One person, by taking a first step, can make a tremendous difference in his or her community.

Chapter Twenty-Two

Learn from Losing

There is only one thing worse than losing—not learning from your loss. Losing is part of politics. Someone wins—someone loses. No one wants to lose when they enter a political campaign. Unfortunately, someone has to. In fact, in most elections where there are multiple candidates for an office, all but one of the candidates lose. In a city council race in Southern California there was a race with nine candidates, only one won. The other eight lost. All thought they had a good chance of winning.

Taking the time after a loss to figure out what happened and what could have been done better is time well spent. Those who take the time to learn from their losses gain valuable insight and knowledge. Ronald Reagan lost the Republican nomination for President before he was eventually successful. Bill Clinton lost a race for governor. George W. Bush was unsuccessful in his attempt to run for congress. Each learned valuable lessons that they were later able to apply to their successful efforts.

Our company has won hundreds of elections, and we have also lost a few, but we learn more from the elections we lose than the ones we win. It is hard to make the time and effort to analyze an election loss and it is often painful, but it is important to do so.

Most analyses of elections usually focus on the winners: what they did, what they said, how they spent their money, what messages voters apparently responded to, or how TV or mail influenced the election. *Campaigns and Elections,* the nations most widely read publication for political consultants, contains article after article, interview after interview with winning consultants who boast about their marvelous strategy and glorious wins. Awards are given for the "best" mail, ads, and posters (whether or not they resulted in victories).

Rarely does anyone want to talk about losses. Losses are to be avoided, hidden, not talked about. Failures are "un-American," a blemish on the otherwise stellar reputation of the consultant or the candidate. No one wants to think about rejection, or even worse, go through the painful process of finding out why voters rejected him. But if you want to improve your chances for success in a future campaign, you must analyze your loss. That is why I try to conduct "post mortems" after every election, win or lose.

After a win, people are eager to get together to bask in the glory and to re-live the experience. Often it is difficult to find and to focus on things that did not work. Wins tend to taint our perception of reality. When you win, and are flushed with success, everything seems to have worked well. For instance, after a win, a typical campaign assessment meeting may lead to comments like:

"We had great mail."

"Our TV spots were on target."

"Our message resonated with voters."

"Our poll was right on target."

"Our campaign team was professional and focused."

"People worked hard."

"I knew we were going to win when the lawn signs went up."

It is possible that all these things are true. It is also possible that luck played a role or that the opposition was incompetent and made serious mistakes. After a successful election, people may overrate the importance and effectiveness of the different elements that went into the campaign. For instance, maybe the mail was good but not great; maybe the TV spots were just acceptable, not really on target. Possibly the poll was overrated and relied upon too much. Maybe the campaign team was inexperienced and ineffective, and just maybe the win was more a fluke than the result of successful campaigning.

Unfortunately, no one will ever know which factors really contributed most to the winning because the glow of success blocks out a realistic assessment of what worked and what did not. A good rule of thumb to remember is this:

You are never as smart as you think you are when you win
or as bad as people say you are when you lose.

* * * * *

Winning can cloud your thinking. Recently I spoke to a conference of community college leaders about passing tax elections. During a question and answer session, a representative of a community college spoke about the recent success her college had in passing a bond measure. This was the third time her district had attempted to pass a bond, and it passed this time by a 57% "yes" vote. She proudly boasted about the victory and described to the conference attendees their campaign strategy of registering students to vote and involving them in the campaign. She went on and on: "This campaign was so much better than the last one, which we lost. This time we got the students involved, and we focused on absentee voters."

Unfortunately, in her enthusiasm about the victory, she missed the real reason why the second campaign won and the previous one had failed. The success was not due to running a better campaign but rather a change in the state law lowering the threshold for passing bond measures from 66.7% to 55%. What she did not recognize was that while the campaign for the previous measure had lost, it had in fact achieved a **63% "yes" vote for the bond, 6%** *more* **than the "winning" campaign.** Perception clouds reality.

* * * * *

Many of our candidate clients have lost elections before hiring us. Some have lost several times. They often have no idea why. Taking time after a loss to reassess one's motivations for running can improve a candidate's focus and commitment. I met with a new client—let's call him Jim—in his law office a few months after he had lost an election for city council. I asked Jim the standard questions about what he felt had gone wrong.

"Do you have any idea why you lost?" I asked.

Like many losing clients, he was unclear. "I worked hard," he said. "I raised more money than my opponent. I went to every forum. I had great looking mail. I had the support of all the unions. I thought our message was clear. By all rights, I should have won."

"So why didn't you?" I asked.

"I have no idea. Perhaps my opponent was better liked than I thought." Jim responded, looking puzzled.

"OK, then," I said, "let's look more closely at just what happened. Let's start at the beginning so we can figure out what went wrong, and more importantly, what you should do if you decide to run again."

I began with some questions to get him looking more closely at his motivation for running for office. I asked him: "What motivates you to make the effort to run? Why do you believe you would do a better job than your opponent? In what ways is your opponent better than you? In what respects are you better? What do you want to accomplish on the city council? Do you have ambition for higher office? Why?"

These were not easy questions. It would have been easier to talk about strategy and how we should proceed to find the votes necessary to win. We could have discussed how we would raise money or talked about the great ads we were going to create.

More important than developing a campaign strategy was learning what was in his heart and belly—why did he want to be elected and what would he do in office if he were elected? Was he willing to make the sacrifices necessary to win? We talked for several hours but never discussed the previous campaign. Only when he had articulated his motivations for running did we begin to talk about the last campaign and about what worked and what had not.

Out of our discussions, we realized that he needed to talk to voters to find out why they had voted for his opponent. We also determined that he needed to be more involved in neighborhood issues that he cared about, regardless of his political ambition. We learned that his supporters really did not do a lot of work for him although they had raised money. Jim readily acknowledged that his "platform" had been developed by him and his closest friends without much input from voters. We learned that it was too complex and too "global" for a campaign for city council. We learned that although Jim spent a lot of money on mail that "looked good," voters thought he appeared too polished.

Through this painful yet productive analysis, Jim learned a lot about his motivation and goals. In the end, we had both learned some new things. He was ready to learn from his mistakes and try again.

* * * * *

A few weeks after suffering a disheartening defeat for a $15 million bond measure, the Hawthorne Unified School District in Southern California asked me to analyze why the measure had failed. The common wisdom was that the tax was too high. The press and local elected city officials criticized the school district for asking for more money than people could afford. Some critics said the district did not need additional funds.

I started by visiting the schools in the district, and it was clear that the district had significant needs. The aging buildings were crowded. Storage rooms were being converted into temporary classrooms and counseling rooms because of the lack of instructional space. To develop a plan to pass a bond, we needed to know more. Why did the previous measure lose? Was it really the size of the bond or the tax rate? Or was it something about the way campaign had been managed? It took several days and numerous meetings with campaign leaders to find out what really happened. After the painful analysis, we realized that the campaign had failed not because of the size of the bond or the amount of the tax but because there was a lack of volunteer support and lack of preparation by the district. Campaign leaders candidly answered the following questions:

Q. "Were voters aware of the renovations that were going to take place in the schools?"

A. "No, we really didn't know ourselves. We wanted to get the money before we developed the plan."

Q. "How many volunteers worked on the campaign?"

A. "We didn't have any volunteers. We hired a company to make phone calls."

Q. "How many people were you expecting to vote?"

A. "We didn't know, we focused on parents."

Q. "Did non-parents support your efforts?

A. "We avoided communicating to non-parents."

It was obvious that the problem was more than the tax rate and that the district would have to rethink its approach if it was to pass a new bond measure.

Over the next year, we worked with a new superintendent of schools to develop a specific plan to improve each school. Parents and teachers participated in developing the plan. Voters in the community—parents *and* non-parents— were provided information about the conditions of the schools and the plans to renovate them. Once the measure was placed on the ballot, a campaign plan was developed that accurately estimated the number of votes needed to win. A campaign team was established and people were encouraged to walk precincts and talk to voters—not just parents.

After 12 months of work, the community eventually passed a school bond which was almost twice the amount previously sought and at a considerably higher tax rate than the one voters had rejected earlier. By analyzing their failed effort, a better plan was developed—one that had the support of voters in the district.

* * * * *

Losing provides an opportunity for learning and improving IF time is taken to analyze the loss. It rarely is. Campaign offices are cleaned up and often closed before a thoughtful analysis is done. Without a careful analysis of what worked and what did not, it is tempting to say everything was bad, and that is not always the case. Failure is part of the political process. Learning from failure is essential. Do not expect different results if you do the same thing the same way.

In politics, losses provide the best learning opportunities. After a loss, minds are more open to discover weaknesses and to identify poor performance. While it may be therapeutic to blame the loss on the opposition, it does more good to look at your own performance. Not everything was done poorly. Some things worked and others did not.

- How could mail be improved? Might it have been too abstract or too detailed to persuade voters?
- How was the timing of the mail delivery to voters? Should the delivery go out sooner or later next time?
- Did we accurately estimate turnout?
- Did we work as hard as we could have?
- Did we lose because of lack of effort, lack of money or because our opposition did a better job? What did they do that was better?
- What did we do well? Why do we think that? What evidence is there?
- Did we have enough time? Did we peak at the right time?
- Did volunteers receive adequate training and supervision?
- Was our message clear?
- Did we stay on message?

A common tendency of losing candidates and campaign staff is to think that something beyond their control was responsible for their loss (such as the opposition having more money). It is also common for losing campaigns to be overly critical of their own effort, thinking everything they did was bad, resulting in a "terrible" campaign. Neither is usually accurate. Post-election evaluations can provide valuable insight as to what worked and what did not. Everyone involved in the campaign should have a chance to reflect on what happened, provide input on what was done right and what went wrong.

Every year, the NCAA conducts a postseason basketball tournament. The top 64 teams in the country are selected to participate. With a one game elimination, only one team out of the 64 ends their season with a win. The players of the losing teams are disappointed, some are too despondent to talk. But out of the losses new determination arises: a commitment "to be back next year," a rededication to work harder, eliminate mistakes, practice more, understand the sacrifice it takes to win. Politics is the same. A loss merely provides an opportunity for growth and improvement.

Remember that the only losers are the people who do not try. If you lose, reflect on what you did well and what could have been improved. After you reflect and learn from your mistakes, look for an opportunity to try again.

Chapter Twenty-Three

The Campaign Never Ends

When we were hired by a school district in a large suburban area, the superintendent instructed me that he wanted to do *one* tax measure in his career and that we better be successful the first time. The superintendent, like many others, had no desire to run another campaign and was adamant this one would be his first and his last. It was not. Our first successful effort which provided basic improvements to the schools, inspired parents and supporters to place a new measure on the ballot three years later. The second measure which provided for new schools and improved facilities, also passed. The superintendent learned what elected officials also learn—that an election victory should be seen as the beginning, not the end.

So much emphasis is placed on "winning" it is easy to forget the reasons for running in the first place. A candidate we successfully worked with gleefully announced on Election Night that he wanted to start running for re-election that very night. He asked for our help in developing a four-year campaign plan. I told him to save his money. The best campaign plan would be for him to do a good job in the position he had just been elected to serve. If he could do that, the re-election campaign would take care of itself. We suggested that he invest in making sure the public was made aware of what he was doing in office and to share with the public his successes as well as his frustrations.

A smart elected official is aware of the need to continually keep the public aware and involved in decisions and projects that affect their lives. If they don't, the public is likely to turn on them. Recently in Oakland, California, the city council voted to double parking fines for vehicles parking in residential areas on street sweeping days. There was no community input, no discussion of whether the street sweepers were effective or not, no communication from the city officials that the fines were to be increased or why. Most people felt the fine increase was merely a way to increase city revenue.

The public was outraged. Our candidate for city council promptly jumped on this issue, and we sent letters to voters in the community asking them to sign a petition opposing the increase. Hundreds of people responded and flooded the city with angry calls. The result was the parking fine was reduced, but not before the public raked city officials over the coals.

Had elected officials taken the time to communicate with the public and gain input, not only would the issue have been resolved easily, but elected officials may also have learned something from the public about the quality of street sweeping and how the service could be improved. Ongoing communications and ongoing efforts to involve people in decisions that affect their lives should not end on Election Day.

Most terms of office are four years—1,460 days to make a difference, to accomplish something. The goal should not be to get re-elected. The goal should be to do something while in office that improves the quality of life in a community. Voting on legislation is one small part of the work. Think about how much you could accomplish if you just accomplished one good thing every day. Getting elected to office is not an end; it is a beginning and an opportunity to make a difference.

More than half of the school districts we now work with have previously passed bond measures and are now asking voters to approve funds to complete additional projects. Public officials are learning that a campaign is really never over. Each election breeds additional work with the community. Smart public officials continually inform their community of projects and how tax dollars are being spent.

Prior to and during an election campaign, most public agencies wisely make great efforts to communicate to the public. Questionnaires and surveys are sent to residents asking their opinion of projects and priorities. At public forums district personnel provide detailed information on how money will be spent. Often voters are encouraged to visit the schools or public facilities that will be improved. We once encouraged voters to visit the Oakland Zoo,

Museum, and Science and Technology Center to see how their tax money was being spent. The motivation? We assumed that informed voters would be supportive voters. The more information we could provide to help them make an informed decision, the better.

It is rare for public officials to maintain the same level of communication with citizens that they did during the campaign. I would argue that it is even more vital after an election that they do so. Once the election is over, the real work begins. Promises made during the heat of the campaign need to be kept. Keeping the public informed is smart strategy.

When the Manhattan Beach Unified School District passed their *first* bond measure, the district made a major effort to keep the public informed about the progress of the projects, problems that arose and the impact of the new facilities (including the disruption caused by construction) on the students. Describing the renovations as Phase One, the district laid an important foundation for another bond measure in the future. Regular communications were sent to parents and non-parents. When new or newly renovated facilities were opened, the public was invited to attend. The superintendent sent letters to the community, and community members were encouraged to participate on committees to plan future improvements. New residents to the community were sent information so they would understand how these new facilities came about. In short, the district used the foundation of support during the first election campaign to build support for the next one, although no one knew at the time when it would occur.

The foresight of the district leaders and the willingness of the Board of Education to "invest" in communicating to the public laid the foundation for another successful bond measure to complete the work that was needed.

The end of the day on Election Day is often a relief. It marks the end of a long campaign of work. People are tired, and few of them want to continue to invest the time and effort. While it may be impossible to continue with the same intensity or pace, it is important to continue to keep people involved and informed.

During a successful campaign for mayor, our staff had weekly meetings with volunteers to involve them in the campaign. Our candidate, impressed with the power of volunteers, promised to keep meeting with them once he was elected. On Election Night, the candidate looked at the crowd, many of whom had volunteered countless hours and said, "I want to thank each of you for your efforts, and I promise we will continue to work together. We will continue to meet as we did on the campaign to make progress for this city."

That was the last time the candidate, now the mayor, met with his volunteers. Four years later, he tried to re-create the enthusiasm and dedication he had benefited from during his first campaign. Calls were made to the old volunteers attempting to relight the fires that had once burned. People were polite and kind, but they remembered his promise to "continue to work together … and we will continue to meet." The mayor had abandoned his supporters for four years, and there was no way they could be persuaded to become as involved as they once had been. He became a one-term mayor.

The election, it turned out, was more about *his* ambition than a desire to empower people. For him the campaign *ended* on Election Night. Had he been wiser and realized that "the campaign never ends" his legacy would have been much greater (and his term of office longer). Whether you are elected to one term, two terms or more, the goal should not be to get reelected, the goal should be to make a difference.

Chapter Twenty-Four

Make a Difference

Working on a political campaign is one important way to make a difference in your community. But even if you are not interested in working on a political campaign, there are many other ways to become involved and to get your voice heard.

If you have a local concern, such as needing a stop sign, a speed bump, a creek cleaned up, or more police patrols, get 11-20 other people to join your effort. Write individual letters to elected officials, and make phone calls to follow-up. Visit your local elected official's office as well. Demand to see the elected official not her aide.

Be a pest, or if you like a more polite word, be persistent. Keep writing, keep calling and keep organizing. Do not let anyone ignore you, and be ready to volunteer to help solve a problem. Do not expect an elected official to do it all for you. If your street is dirty, grab a broom. Better yet, get your neighbors to join you. Do not wait for others to act. Most importantly, get off your butt! Things will not get better if you expect others to do it.

Follow the seven Sidewalk Strategies to make a difference. Take personal responsibility. Work hard. Listen. Know what it takes to win. Keep things simple. Be willing to volunteer. Do not quit.

Make a difference with your life. Do not be afraid of failing or of making mistakes. Volunteer on a political campaign or an effort to improve your neighborhood or community. Our democracy is dependent on people becoming involved. We need to encourage people to serve on school boards, hospital boards and water boards. Volunteers are an essential part of a healthy democracy and a vibrant community.

How can you get your voice heard? Can you get elected leaders to listen? It happens every day as long as people take initiative to make a difference. Apartheid in South Africa was ended partly by the pressure of political activists and church leaders around the world. The banning of DDT and other toxic chemicals occurred after Rachel Carson wrote *Silent Spring* which also prompted the eventual legislation that created the Environmental Protection Agency.

Farm workers in California gained the right to unionize, not because of the benevolence of elected officials or growers, but because the public demanded it. Jimmy Carter has made a greater impact as a private citizen than he did as President of the most powerful nation in the world. He has become a role model for people young and old through his volunteer efforts to build housing, his efforts to promote peace and understanding, and his efforts to wipe out disease.

An important thing to recognize is that, unfortunately, most elected officials, Democrats and Republicans alike, do not *lead*. They *follow*. There are, of course, exceptions but not many. If you want to make change, you need to recognize that your audience is not elected officials but the people. Elected officials are far less important than they think they are. Get enough people to take action, and the elected officials will follow.

* * * * *

My son, Michael, spent a summer as in intern at the White House. He worked in the White House "Office of Correspondence." He was one of 30 or so students from around the country who had the political connections to be selected to work over the summer as an unpaid intern. He spent three months in Washington, D.C. working in the Old Executive Office Building responding to the thousands of letters the White House receives daily.

He had his picture taken with the First Lady and met the Vice President. He suffered through the humid heat of the summer in Washington. He was exposed to columnist and talk show host Chris Mathews and attended a briefing by Clinton advisor James Carville. But mostly, he learned a lot about how public officials "listen to constituents."

While the White House Office of Correspondence is the biggest of its kind in the capital, it is not unique—each senator and representative has a similar office. In these offices, 22-year-old interns and volunteers sort incoming letters by category then send a form letter back, signed by a machine that duplicates the signature of that representative (or that of the President or First Lady). Letters from constituents are categorized by issue and counted. Form letters are generally disregarded as are postcards and petitions. While an individual letter may not be read by anyone in "power," the cumulative affect of numerous letters is significant.

Years ago, elected officials used town hall meetings to get a handle on public opinion. While today polling provides elected officials with a more precise gauge of public sentiment without the effort of meeting with the public, thousands of letters from angry or concerned constituents can bring attention and action.

At the local level it is even more true. A single well-written letter to a city council member about the need for a stop sign or a speed bump may generate a return call from the council member. Get 10-15 neighbors to write, and chances are they will get a call from the director of public works.

Jane Brunner, an Oakland City Council member, took notice when a constituent called her for assistance in stopping city workers from cutting down a mature tree on her street. When Jane investigated the problem she found that city staff was proposing new guidelines for removing trees, which if implemented, would threaten virtually every street tree in Oakland. (The city logo, ironically, is an oak tree!). Jane went into action and sent a letter to the community asking people to get involved (smartly knowing that a thousand voices are more effective than one). Through Jane's efforts hundreds of citizens became active in the effort to save the trees. These collective efforts forced the city staff to develop new guidelines, and to seek public input, before removal of trees. What started with one person ended with hundreds becoming involved.

Local elected officials, who rely less on polls and more on direct input from constituents, often receive some of their best ideas from "average citizens."

For example, in California, a frustrated citizen, Joan Kiley, who saw her neighborhood deteriorating because of drug dealing and prostitution around a local liquor store, wrote a letter of protest to her city council representative. Her action prompted a new law despite the vehement protests of the liquor and retail store industry lobbyists. The law allowed local communities to pass ordinances making liquor store owners responsible for illegal activities around their liquor stores. Though it started as a neighborhood issue, her letter got the ball rolling, and it snowballed into a state law affecting communities throughout California.

Joan Kiley is not a celebrity. She never ran for office or sought attention or fame. Perhaps some of her neighbors do not even know who she is or what she accomplished, but because she became involved, her neighborhood and her community are better.

There are thousands of Joan Kileys in communities around the country. They are the unsung heroes that make communities better.

In 1954, President Dwight D. Eisenhower wrote: "Politics ought to be the part-time profession of every citizen who would protect the rights and privileges of free people and who would preserve what is good and fruitful in our national heritage."

Garrison Keillor expressed it well, writing in Time Magazine August 25, 2003 "… Most men and women in politics are there because they genuinely like people and want to do good things on their behalf. It's hard work and fury isn't the best motivation. You have to sit through the meetings, listen to other people and say your piece and be civil about it." And later " … You go for a walk on a summer night and notice the little ramps carved into curbs at street corners. People sat through a lot of meetings to get that accomplished. It was a boon to the wheelchair crowd and also to parents pushing strollers and kids riding bikes. It made life slightly more civil and friendly. Government works through small, incremental changes …"

©2003 TIME inc. reprinted by permission.

It is not necessary to be a professional organizer to be effective. It just takes desire and a willingness to put in effort and to become involved in your community. Effective political action rarely happens spontaneously or overnight. Someone must provide the spark. Someone must be willing to take the first steps that lead to bigger steps that eventually lead to change.

Everybody can make a difference *if* they take the first step. Good luck.

Appendix

Basics of Winning Tax Elections

Raising taxes is serious business. People work hard for their money, and asking them to part with some of it through increased taxes should be done only after exhausting all other sources. Raising taxes should be the last resort when trying to pay for important public projects and services.

Public officials often desire additional funds from taxpayers because they do not want to make the tough decisions. For example, school districts do not like to tell sports boosters that a desired stadium will not be supported by voters. Librarians often want a state-of-the-art new library when an extension or remodel of the old library is adequate. The public expects that before they are asked to support a tax increase, that public officials have done their jobs to eliminate waste, and to eliminate projects and programs that are not essential. Rarely will the public be willing to support all the things that need funding. In short, the public has to be convinced that the revenue from a tax measure is really needed, and there is no other way to fund these essential projects or programs.

Our firm has helped public agencies pass over $15 billion in bond measures and other taxes. We have passed parcel taxes, sales taxes and general obligation bonds. We have passed taxes for schools, colleges, transit agencies, museums, libraries, police and fire services, sports facilities, street lighting, zoos, hospitals, sewers, parks, lake clean-ups and acquiring open space. We like to say, "We have helped raise more taxes than anyone in America who is not an elected official." We believe that any school district, college district, hospital district, library, city or county can be successful *if* they take the proper steps.

* * * * *

A wealthy Southern California school district wanted to pass a bond to repair their aging and overcrowded schools. During our initial meeting, I learned that the relatively small district had over $20 million in reserves from the sale of property. These reserves were invested, and interest from this investment was being used to fund various district projects. During our "site visits" to see first hand the needs of the schools, the president of the Board of Education pointed to the glass skylights in several of the classrooms.

"You see those skylights?" she asked. "That's one of the reasons we need to pass this bond measure. If we have an earthquake, shards of glass from the skylights are going fall, and glass is going to fall on the heads of the children underneath!" Pausing for emphasis, she added. "We must pass this bond! The safety of our kids is at stake!"

I looked at her almost incredulously. "Are you telling me that the school district has over $20 million of reserves that you are earning interest on and that you haven't fixed these skylights? You are waiting until the public passes a bond before you fix them? If I was a voter in this district, I'd vote no on your bond," and pausing for emphasis, I added, "and I'd vote to throw you out of office first chance I had!"

Over the next several weeks, we discussed the skylights and other projects that were needed. We decided that before we placed a measure on the ballot, everything that was a critical health and safety issue would be fixed with existing resources before we asked voters to support a tax increase. We also decided to use a significant portion of the district's reserves to reduce the overall cost to taxpayers.

After several months of work and before we asked voters to increase their taxes, we developed a needs list, school by school. Anything that could be fixed using available resources was fixed. Anything that was desired but not essential for improving student achievement we eliminated from our needs. The process was not easy. Parents and teachers were powerful advocates for special programs and needs. We forced ourselves to look at the total long-term needs of the schools and decide whether to renovate existing buildings

Designs courtesy of Jane Norling Designs

Simple images can carry powerful messages

or build new facilities. We wanted to make dramatic improvements in the schools, but we wanted to be reasonable and thoughtful. We made tough decisions and, in the end, developed a plan that met the needs of the students and the district and would hopefully be acceptable to taxpayers. We decided not to go for everything at once, and opted to go for improvements to the elementary schools and the middle school before asking voters for more money for high school improvements.

The election was difficult. We needed 66.7% to win, and we got 68%. Organized opposition tried to punch holes in our plan, but we were able to counter each of their attacks because of the tough decisions we had made months before. The fact that we had fixed things *first* before asking taxpayers for support made sense to elderly voters who were the largest group of voters. Our success in eliminating projects that were desired by parents but not essential impressed people who did not have children in the schools. Decisions made months earlier allowed us to be successful on Election Day.

* * * * *

The most important lesson in passing tax measures is to always remember it is the public's money. Treat it as if it were your own. Do not waste it, do not take it for granted, and do not ask for more than you need. Make sure that every other source of money has been utilized *before* asking the public to support a tax. Elected officials desiring approval of a tax measure have the responsibility to develop the best possible proposal *before* placing a measure on the ballot. That may mean eliminating or postponing projects that are not absolutely essential. It may mean identifying other sources of revenue to reduce the cost to taxpayers. The measure must be well thought out, the need real and the tax acceptable.

While you do not want to be greedy, you also do not want to be overly cautious. Inaction does not solve problems. Some elected officials are opposed to putting *any* measure on the ballot that will increase people's taxes. But allowing people to vote for or against tax increases and to approve or reject taxes for specific purposes is one of the most basic forms of democracy.

Winning tax elections starts with developing a plan for what you want to accomplish with the additional revenue. When I began working with school districts years ago, the common practice was for the school district to first determine through a poll how much voters would be willing to tax themselves. Once the district officials determined this, they then developed a spending plan that was equal to that tax. This is called backing into a plan. A few districts were successful, but many were not. Those that were successful were often disappointed later because the amount of money they were able to get the voters to approve was usually less than what they needed.

Whether you work for a school district needing additional funds for programs or to build or renovate schools; for a hospital district that needs voter support to re-build aging facilities; for a city that faces cutbacks in police and fire services or for any of the countless other public agencies needing the support of taxpayers, the following common sense strategies will greatly improve your chances for voter support:

Common Sense Strategies to Pass a Tax Measure:

Be courageous. If you don't think you can, you won't. If you don't try, you've failed. A school district we have <u>tried</u> to work with for years has never <u>attempted</u> a ballot measure to improve the schools, despite the fact that schools are deteriorating due to lack of funds. Although neighboring school districts have received voter approval for tax measures, this district is "afraid" to ask voters for support. Unfortunately, because school "leaders" are too cautious, the children are continuing to pay the price with inadequate facilities.

Be smart. Before placing a measure on the ballot, write your needs in language that people can understand. Avoid "government-speak," acronyms and technical terms. Make sure that your needs are reasonable, clear and understandable. If you cannot simply state why you need the money, you will not get any. A hospital district we successfully worked with initially thought that voters would approve a tax increase to build a new state-of-the-art hospital. When we saw the architectural drawings we knew we had a problem. The new buildings were indeed state-of-the-art and far more elaborate than the local community would support. We promptly and successfully urged hospital leaders to focus their communications, not on these gleaming new buildings, but on the underlining reason the hospital needed to build new facilities—to make the hospital earthquake safe.

Determine what the public will support. The best plan, if it doesn't make sense to voters, will sit on a shelf unimplemented. In tax elections the public ultimately gets to decide what they want to tax themselves for. A school district in San Diego County failed several times on the ballot attempting to convince the public to build a new second high school to relieve overcrowding. Only after these expensive losses did district officials get the message that the community wanted ONE high school, not two. The district wisely put a measure on the ballot to expand the original high school (even though the tax was higher than the previously failed measures) and won handily.

Make tough decisions. Find other sources of money before asking the public to increase their taxes. We routinely recommend that our clients apply for all funding they may be eligible for BEFORE asking the public to increase their taxes. Make cuts—eliminate waste or needless programs.

Make priorities. Provide the public with evidence that you are making sound decisions *before* asking them for money. Voters in the Oakland Unified School District recently voted to increase their taxes despite the fact that the State of California had taken over administration of the schools because of the district's financial mismanagement. Voters passed the measure, in part because they had been convinced that the district, under state control, was eradicating waste—eliminating cell phone abuse, closing under-utilized schools, and cutting unneeded positions.

Understand who votes. Most of the people who vote probably will not use what the tax will be spent on. Since likely voters generally are older and more conservative than the general population, your needs better make sense to them. The Las Virgenes School District in Southern California passed a parcel tax after volunteers went door-to-door for several months talking to senior citizen voters. Many citizens took advantage of the district's offer of a "senior exemption" so seniors on fixed incomes would not be burdened by the new tax. Although many seniors did not take advantage of this opportunity, they appreciated the fact that volunteers came to their doors to explain it to them.

Determine when you want to be on the ballot. Time is your greatest ally and can be your biggest enemy if you waste it. Before placing a measure on the ballot determine when is the most opportune time *for passage*. Voter turnout varies from election to election. You may benefit from a higher voter turnout or from a lower voter turnout. The important thing is to know which and make decisions accordingly.

Build an army of volunteers. The best political mail in the world or the most effective ads will not be sufficient to win a tax election. Volunteers are the key to success. Make it fun and keep them working toward the goal. (Re-read Chapter Twenty!)

During the course of her three months working as the Coordinator for Fullerton School District's successful Measure CC campaign in conservative Orange County, Hilda Sugarman sent out dozens of email messages to campaign volunteers. They contained words of encouragement and inspiration, an update on the progress towards their goal, and fun news and stories. She also acknowleged errors and problems. Her efforts kept people focused on their goal. Here is a sample:

Subject: First night of Phone Banking

Dear Everyone:

I am so excited that I felt I must report on our first night of phone banking.

38 volunteers got 748 YES VOTES!!!!

We only need to get another 14,252 votes to win!!!!!!

Mark kept the night fun with his FABULOUS rewards. A prize for the phone person first to get 20 YES votes. A prize for the most yes vote getter of the evening. In between "hugs & kisses," Pez and puns. Thursday night is a fun night!! . . . .

Subject: Wednesday

Happy Wednesday!!! We are back in the money again.

Our phone banking ran into a glitch on Tuesday night. We co-coordinators owe Tuesday nighters a hug for trying and "I am sorry" for not having the lists you needed. WE REALLY ARE SORRY!!! You were great sports!!

YOU all worked your ears off!! Thank you. With little to work on, WEDNESDAY night once again astounded even the most ardent believer with 351 yes votes!!!!! Their 2 night total tops a thousand!!!!! Once again Markie posted his chart to let the gang know just how well they were doing. First they got flags for significant milestones. Then erasers and pencils. Boy do Wednesday nighters get turned on by this good stuff!!! It's a Pavlovian group to be sure!!!

Bob even used the cell phone to get a couple of YES votes from people from his school that have CALL BLOCKING. No one is safe from BOB the UNBLOCKER!! . . . .

Subject: You have been waiting to hear this

Fyi: we are **NOW** at 8368 yes votes!

That means we are half way to our magic number - 15,000!

33 days to get $50 million!!!

Subject: One month left

Hi Everyone!

Just to let you know: We are coming into our last month of working for $50,000,000.

Our phone bankers have been doing a fabulous job.

Monday night 25 wonderful people found 298 yes votes!!! It was a tough list and you came through!!!

We are getting closer to our target - 15,000.

Thank you Tuesday NIGHTERS!!! We got 324 YES people from our hardest support group - MEN. This list wasn't just men, but men without children in our schools. Republican and Independent men. Some of that group are even on fixed income. JUST A JAMIN' Job!!!

Subject: Happy Friday

We are moving toward 11,000 YES VOTES!!! . . . .

As disappointed as I was, I was unable to phone bank tonight, Thursday night. Fortunately, a mole at the phone banks reported to me:

It seems that our own dear, sweet Gaye was doing her calling in her usual diligent manner. She got a sweet woman and asked the usual question. The lady said she was voting YES. Gaye, being on top of her game, then asked the lady if her husband would vote yes. The woman responded, "Sure he will, he has a brain injury and will do what I tell him to." What a lovely couple!!!

Dan receives the metal of the week for perseverance in phone banking. After you hear his stick-to-it -ness you will certainly agree:
Mild mannered Dan called an elderly "gentleman" in his 80's. The man answered the phone by saying, "Speak up A__ -Hole." So, probably speaking up, Dan started talking to the gent about CC. The man said " I have no money" and hung up. Our hero, Dan, called the gentleman back to explain that we were just giving out information. Again, when the man answered the phone by saying "Speak up A__-Hole." Now Dan explained about measure CC and the man said that he would vote YES!

That man sure has a different way to answer the phone. Maybe its a thing about being free to do what you want when you're 80. Or maybe this man was really 14 and home alone! But if he is over 21, we all really like him.

Subject: $50,000,000 - One more day!

Hi my friends,

In 21 hours this election will be over. However the wonderful friendships we have formed will continue. We have all learned a lot in these past 2 months. From my heart I thank each of you for your generous gifts of time, money and support. . . . . .

After polls close at 8:00pm we can watch the results come in, together, at Ching Ting Restaurant. Hope to see you there and personally thank you for your efforts. . . . .

Subject: **WOW! VICTORY!**

Dear Friends

In an election where the most conservative candidates won, your dedication and hard work pulled out a victory. Not just a squeaky victory, a clear victory - a bold statement of support from our community.. . . . . . Your perseverance and positive attitudes clearly communicated the needs of our schools to our voters. They asked appropriate questions and responded by reaching into their pocketbooks to improve our schools, support the technology education of our students and provided needed classroom space. They want the same things we want for our students. How awesome that is!

Further, the interaction between parents,administrators, staff, classified employees, board members and community will make a significant positive impact on the effectiveness of our schools for years to come. I hope that one IMPORTANT lesson we have each learned is the need to maintain those ties with colleagues and others.

A special thank you to your bond committee: Their dedication and vision for a better future for our community made this campaign successful.

This is a fabulous day!!!

Get the resources you need. Managing election campaigns has become increasingly complicated and expensive, but there are numerous resources to help. Determine who will benefit from the measure if it passes. Develop a budget, and then approach each group or individual with a request for a specific amount. Do not be shy or embarrassed. Be straightforward and honest. Ask for what you need. Political campaigns need funds, and those who will benefit if it is successful should be asked to contribute.

Finally, if at first you don't succeed, don't be afraid to try again. You don't give up on baseball if you strike out the first time. You don't give up trying to drive if you failed the DMV test. You don't stop cooking when your first cake flops, so why would you stop asking voters for support if your first or even second attempt failed? More public agencies failed once before succeeding than those that won the first time out. If you don't take the first step, you'll never get anywhere.

* * * * *

In many states, passage of tax measures require a simple majority vote. Despite this, many tax measures still fail to get public support. In studying why tax measures failed we found a number of common mistakes that if avoided can improve your chances of passing a tax measure.

Common Mistakes Public Agencies Make When Trying to Pass a Tax Measure:

Lack of strong, committed leadership with a single-minded focus. If the leaders of the organization are not completely and totally behind the measure and are not willing to sacrifice time and effort for passage, it is unlikely that the measure will pass. Leadership starts at the top. Behind most successful measures is a strong, able leader.

"Let's do it ourselves." In a desire to save money, or out of sheer arrogance, many districts try to pass the tax measure without outside help. While noble, these efforts generally lack sophistication on setting tax rates, developing a proposal the public will support and communicating to the voters who are most likely to vote. There is a lot of help and expertise available. Use it! The cost of procuring expert help is minimal when compared to the cost of losing an election and having to do it all over again. After the affluent community of Piedmont rejected a series of taxes to maintain city services, I was asked to assess why voters rejected the measures. The measures would have generated tens of millions of dollars over the life of the taxes. The city had decided not to commission a poll to determine an acceptable tax rate or to discover what programs were important to citizens and which were not. I asked a prominent architect who was on the tax committee if he would ever build a building, costing tens of millions of dollars, without developing a plan based on research. "Absolutely not!" he replied. But that is exactly what they did by moving forward without conducting a poll. The election losses could have been avoided by a bit of advice and research early on.

"Give us the money first, then we'll develop the plan." As bizarre as it sounds, I have heard this on many occasions. Not wanting to invest time or money in developing a plan, some public agencies will put a measure on the ballot first hoping for passage, after which they promise to develop a specific plan. They usually fail.

Inability to eliminate projects or programs that are not absolutely necessary. A case could be made for almost any improvement in schools or projects that serve the public. Rest assured that there is a built-in interest group that wants something (and they usually want someone else to pay for it). Whether it is an Olympic-sized pool, a new weight room or additional classrooms, there will be someone who will say the need is essential. The public should not be asked to support a wish list of projects. Paring down the needs list (and consequently the tax) to the essentials helps to build credibility and support from the public. The Los Altos-Mountain View High School District failed THREE times before eliminating projects that voters felt unnecessary. By eliminating lights for the stadium and building a new wrestling room (both items vigorously desired by the sports boosters) the district demonstrated frugality and common sense and the voters responded favorably.

Not taking time to plan well or build support. No one would think of building a house without having solid plans. Yet, many public agencies put tax measures on the ballot without proper preparation. We normally advise our clients to take at least six months to one year to develop a plan and to build support *before* they place a measure on the ballot.

Not raising sufficient resources to be able to campaign effectively. No public funds may be used to convince voters to raise their taxes. All campaign funds need to be raised privately from people and organizations that support the ballot measure. Unfortunately, campaigns require financial resources that should be identified *before* the measure is placed on the ballot.

Insufficient volunteer commitment. Unlike other types of elections that are won primarily in the media or through paid advertising of one variety or another, tax measures usually require a strong commitment from volunteers who are able to convince neighbors to raise their taxes. Volunteers are also able to put a human face on the request for funds. In most tax elections, the people who provide services (teachers, nurses, librarians, fire fighters) or those who receive services (parents, patients) are the most persuasive proponents. Without volunteers tax measures fail.

Campaigning on behalf of the public agency as opposed to specific projects the tax will benefit. Voters are not likely to support an additional tax that benefits a public agency like a school district, transit district or hospital district unless the needs are spelled out specifically. Voters are more likely to support proposals to renovate *specific schools, pay for adding additional bus lines or save an emergency room.* A "district" is merely another government agency. It is far better to articulate the *programs* or the specific *projects* the tax will benefit. The point is to be specific as to the beneficiaries of the tax rather than talk about the agency that will administer the money.

Focusing on the money not the need. No prudent advertiser focuses on the cost of an item over the benefit that will be derived from it. We recently passed a $350 million bond measure for the San Juan Unified School District. Initially, the local newspaper led every article with the tag line "… the $350 million bond measure, which is the largest bond measure in the history of the Central Valley." We worked to explain to the reporter and the newspaper that while what they were saying was accurate, the reason it was so large was the district was large. In fact, smaller districts had passed bond measures that were far bigger proportionately given the number of schools the bond measure was to help, and our tax rate was smaller. Eventually, the reporter "got" what we were saying and changed the way she started each article. Had the measure been defined as the "$350 million bond" instead of "the bond to repair and renovate our local schools" we may have lost.

Conferences. Attend and listen, but don't believe everything you hear. One of the best ways to learn what others have done to be successful is to attend conferences featuring presentations by people who have passed successful tax measures. But if you do attend, be prepared to ask tough questions.

Conferences that cater to public officials are a multi-million dollar business. There are conferences for school board members, school business officials, superintendents, teachers, librarians, health care officials, elected city council members, city managers and transit district officials. The conferences are in each state, and there are also national conferences. Thousands of people pay significant sums of money to attend these conferences, to network and to learn everything from running tax elections to finding the best scuff resistant floor coverings. There are seminars for people wanting to know how to access more state dollars, seminars for new superintendents, for nurses and for financial planners. There are conferences for new elected officials and for representatives of low wealth and high wealth communities. Topics cover every imaginable issue.

Companies wanting to make money selling products or services to public agencies, covet opportunities to conduct seminars and workshops at these conferences. Financial advisory and underwriting firms, legal advisors and pollsters provide their expertise and advice to public institutions. It is a great way for them to reach potential new clients and obtain new business. I know I always try to make a presentation on winning tax elections, as do my competitors.

Usually, the presentations on tax elections follow the same pattern. A consultant, fresh off of an impressive victory with the assistance of a board member or superintendent eager to impart some wisdom to others, spends an hour or so answering fairly routine questions about winning tax measures. Handouts are provided, listing other satisfied clients as well as a few tips for winning. Attendees are looking for insights and strategies, and these seminars provide valuable assistance to them. In the evening, architects, attorneys and the financial advisors host dinners and receptions for attendees. Thousands of dollars are spent hosting conference attendees for one simple reason: There is money to be made in tax elections. How much? No one tells you.

I have often wondered what I would ask if I was in the audience. Would I ask how much money the attorneys, financial advisors and architects make on the projects? Would I ask whether it is always essential to have a poll? What do they cost? Would I be bold enough to ask whether the involvement of elected officials in the campaign is good or bad? Since all presenters talk about their winning efforts, and tax measures often lose, would I be courageous enough to ask which elections they lost? Would they be honest and say?

Here are some of the answers to the questions no one ever seems to ask:

1. How to choose a legal advisor? Tax election law is a somewhat unique field. Make sure the legal advisor you choose has broad experience in tax election law and has experience working with similar clients with similar needs. Ask other agencies who they use and why. Do your homework.

What do they cost? For bond elections, most legal advisors work on contingency, which means they get paid only if the election is successful. Do not confuse contingency with free. Attorneys and others use contingency for marketing purposes and to mask at the beginning of the process what their fees are. Often, both legal advisors and financial advisors charge a percent or a fraction of a percent of the total amount of the bonds issued. A half of a percent sounds small, but it could be thousands of dollars. Like the old saying says: "Everything is negotiable." Ask how much (in dollars, not percentages) they will make. If your bond measure will have a number of issuances you will pay each time. Ask questions. Remember, you *can* negotiate.

2. Do you need a poll? Probably, but not always. Polls are helpful to determine tax rates and projects the public will support. Polls taken months before an election are less useful than those taken close to an election. A poll done without the input of the person who will eventually manage the campaign is less valuable. A poll done by a firm that has a financial interest in the outcome (financial advisor) should not be trusted.

What do polls cost? Depending on the length of the poll, anywhere from $15,000 to $30,000. One word of caution: Some financial advisors and consultants use the lure of "free polls" to land unsuspecting clients. These "free polls" are usually just a marketing ploy to get their foot in the door. If someone is offering something free, question its validity and rest assured the firm offering the free service is going to make money somewhere down the line.

3. How to choose a financial advisor? There are financial advisors and there are underwriters. Financial advisors advise the district on various financial options and costs associated with the tax election, and selling of bonds afterwards if the tax election is about bonds. They may help the public agency sell the bonds. Underwriters may also advise the public agency on financial matters, they may help sell the bonds, and they may purchase the bonds to sell to others. Sounds complicated but is really not. In choosing a financial advisor or underwriter, experience and reputation are the two most important qualities. Again, ask your colleagues in other districts who they use and why. Experience is more important than fancy marketing brochures.

What do financial advisors cost? Like the legal advisors, most financial advisors work "on contingency," which again, means they get paid only if the measure is successful. This also means they are making some healthy fees down the line. Ask what they will get paid. Get real dollars, not percentages. Percentages can mask the cost to the district. Costs vary from one district to the next. It also depends whether your bond sale is a one time event or whether there will be multiple sales. Remember they make money on every transaction. The more they make, the less money is available for your projects. Find out how much your financial advisor will get paid.

4. How involved should local elected officials be in the effort? The public agency that puts a tax measure on the ballot should be convinced prior to doing so that there is public support for doing so. Elected officials should be involved as long as they are not operating in their official elected status. They are not. Tax elections are very different. The biggest problem is that elected officials usually think they are experts in elections because they were elected to office. Tax elections are very different.

5. How to choose a political advisor? The lines between political advisors/financial advisors/planners/legal advisors/pollsters are becoming blurred. The reason—money. Our advice is to select a political advisor who is not involved with selling other services to the district. That means avoiding political advisors who will make money on construction or selling the bonds. Previous experience is the best indicator of future success.

How much do they cost? Most political advisors charge between $30,000 and $65,000.

6. What about "free" services? No reputable financial advisor, polling firm, or political advisor will provide these services for free. "Free" services are often used to obtain other more profitable work. BEWARE.

7. How do you finance your election? Elections have three major phases. First is the planning phase, second is the campaign phase and third is the post-election phase. During the planning phase, the public agency may spend resources doing a needs assessment of facilities or programs. Often, the analysis that is done at this stage will provide important information to determine whether or not to pursue a tax election. Facilities and programs can be assessed and costs determined. Possible financial options can be considered. It is even possible to do polling to determine whether or not the public is supportive of the plan and if not, why. Communications to citizens may also be sent informing them of the conditions or needs of the agency.

After the agency puts a measure on the ballot, no public money or resources may be spent advocating or supporting the measure. This phase must be funded by private contributions to the campaign. Financial contributors are often those that will benefit from passage of the measure.

Construction firms, financial advisors (where it is legal to do so), architects and others often contribute to electoral campaigns.

8. What do we do once we pass our measure? Once the measure passes (or fails), the agency may again communicate to voters on how the money is being spent or what the needs are. Often this post-election communication outreach work is not done, and the agency loses a lot of support it once had with voters. Keep communicating. Keep working.

My name is Devon Bates and I'm a third grader at Toyon Elementary School.

I'm writing to ask you to vote Yes on Measure B to help repair our Berryessa schools.

I think that if people know how the money is going to be spent they would all vote for Measure B.

I'd like to show you some of the reasons why Measure B is so important for our schools.

The teachers at our school are great, but our school is really old.

Political mail doesn't have to be "slick" to be effective. This young student explained the need for a bond measure simply and effectively.

Our school was built
55 years ago. Some of
our schools need repair
to make them
earthquake safe.

Our custodian
does the best he
can to keep the
school clean, but
there are some
things he can't
even fix. The
drinking fountains
are disgusting.
Measure B will repair
bathrooms and fix
leaky roofs.

When our schools were built in the 1950s and 1960s, they didn't have computers like we use today. There aren't enough plugs and cords are all over the room.

Measure B will replace broken windows and renovate our classrooms.

Sincerely,
Devon Bates

P.S. My mom and dad say one of the reasons they are voting for Measure B is that all the money raised stays right here for Berryessa kids.

Larry Tramutola is a 30-year veteran of political and community organizing. He is often quoted in the *San Francisco Chronicle*, *Los Angeles Times*, *San Jose Mercury News* and the *Bond Buyer* for his political insight and expertise. He is married to Ann Caponio Tramutola, and they have four children. Larry is a graduate of Stanford University.

Contact Larry or the TRAMUTOLA COMPANY at
www.TRAMUTOLA.com

What People Are Saying About
Sidewalk Strategies...

"Public officials and commissioners, school and hospital administrators should have a copy of this book handed to them to be kept under their pillow the way Alexander the Great kept a copy of The Iliad under his. Obviously anyone with an ambition to change the world through the practice of democracy needs to read this book, but it's also a good read for anyone working with groups of people."

Newtopia Magazine

"As I read Sidewalk Strategies I found myself saying over and over—'I really wish people who do organizing ... would read this book.' Now that you know about it, read it."

Randy Shaw, Author, The Activist Handbook

"Larry Tramutola probably won't end up on a stamp, like his mentor, Cesar Chavez, but having orchestrated more than 400 election wins and more than $15 billion in community-improvement tax measures, his résumé isn't too shabby. His appropriately named Sidewalk Strategies: Seven Winning Steps for Candidates, Causes and Communities ... is a challenge to would-be power brokers and ego trippers... The anecdotes make this book as much an inside look at California political history as a campaign guide."

San Francisco Bay Guardian

"This is a great book for those that want to organize political or other campaigns on the local level. It stresses political organizing the old fashioned way—getting people involved at the grassroots level to bring about change. It uses the principles of community organizing developed by Fred Ross and implemented by Cesar Chavez and the United Farm Workers. The author, trained under both, is a very successful political campaign organizer who has refined these people-to-people campaign techniques for today's campaigns."

Andy Coe, Government/Community Relations, Stanford University

"Sidewalk Strategies is a roadmap of strategies for winning campaigns."

Dolores Huerta, Co-Founder, United Farm Workers;
Regent, University of California

Printed in the United States
37691LVS00006B/121